PERSECUTION

OF THE

LUTHERAN CHURCH

IN PRUSSIA,

FROM THE YEAR 1831, TO THE PRESENT TIME;

COMPILED FROM GERMAN PUBLICATIONS.

CHIEFLY TRANSLATED BY J. D. LÖWENBERG.

(With additional information from various sources.)

I was a stranger, and ye took me in :
I was in prison, and ye came unto me.
MATT. xxv. 35, 36.

LONDON:

PUBLISHED BY HAMILTON, ADAMS, & CO.
JOHN JOHNSTONE, EDINBURGH;
AND WRIGHT & ALBRIGHT, AVON-STREET, BRISTOL.

1840.

TO THE

PROTESTANT CHURCHES

OF

GREAT BRITAIN,

In the confidence, that, seeing their Lutheran Sister has fallen into violent hands, and lies stripped and wounded, they will not, like the Priest and Levite, pass by unmoved, but, for Luther's sake, as well as for that of our Holy Head, who suffers with his Church, will act the part of the good Samaritan, by binding up her wounds, this little volume is respectfully inscribed by

THE COMPILER.

CONTENTS.

	Page
Introduction	vii
Brief Outline of the Persecution, by Pastor Grabau	15
Further Particulars, by C. B. Schulthes	19
Extracts from the Appeal of Pastor Kavel	22
Seizure of the Lutheran Church at Kaulwitz	26
Outrage upon the Church at Hönigern, and Barbarous Treatment of the Congregation	28
Vexatious Proceedings against Baron von Koszutski	35
M. Ernst's History of the Persecution of the Lutheran Church in Prussia	61
King of Prussia's Refusal to receive the Deputation from Silesia	93
Farewell Address of the Emigrants to South Australia	104
Their Admirable Conduct while at Hamburgh	110
Voyage to South Australia	112
High Testimony respecting them, from the South Australian Gazette	142

INTRODUCTION.

In the summer of 1839, a company of interesting strangers, in the German costume, were observed to enter the port of Newcastle-on-Tyne. They stayed there but a few hours, and then proceeded to Liverpool, from whence they were intending to take shipping for North America.

Inquiry was made by the agents of the Bible Society as to their supply of the Holy Scriptures, and most satisfactory answers were elicited. Their deportment was very pleasing, but they appeared to have no letters of introduction to any parties in this country; and little could be learned of their history, excepting that they were Lutheran emigrants, proceeding from the Prussian dominions to the wilds of America, on account of severe persecution for conscience' sake in their native land. A week or two afterwards, another similar company arrived; and was followed by successive parties during the summer months, amounting altogether to about six hundred and forty individuals.*

Public attention was roused, and more minute

---

* Four hundred more passed through England at the same time, by way of Hull.

inquiry was made respecting their circumstances; for " severe persecution for conscience' sake," in the present enlightened age, appeared a new and startling fact. These inquiries have been numerous and particular, and the result unravels a piteous tale of arbitrary and cruel oppression.

For 300 years past, the forefathers of these people have adhered to the creed laid down in the Confession of Augsburg, and have never materially deviated from it. It is well known that this creed not only received the sanction of the champions of our Protestant faith, Luther and Melancthon; but has also been incorporated with the laws of the German Empire, and with various treaties of peace, and other privileges of the State.

For the last twenty years, the Prussian Government has attempted to blend the two existing Protestant churches—the Reformed and the Lutheran—into one; and for the last seven, the most coercive measures have been used to effect this purpose. Heavy fines have been levied continually; and those who were unable to pay them, have been harshly thrown into prison, and allowed to lie there for months, and even years. Their clothing, furniture, cattle, agricultural implements, &c. have been sold, and the parties thus oppressed reduced to the lowest ebb of misery and want.

Few particular details of these sufferings were gained from the emigrants; there was a remarkable absence of bitterness in alluding to their oppressors—seldom or never a murmuring word. But the sickly appearance of many—the grey locks of the reverend old men—the streaming tears of the females—the little infants clasped to their mothers' bosoms—all told but too plainly, that no common, or every-day circumstances, had led to the important step they were taking.

As evening drew on, they were often seen to bow meekly in solemn worship before God, pouring out their sorrows to Him, who will never turn a deaf ear to the cry of the humble. It was striking to witness the cheering effect of such exercises: the aching heart was so evidently relieved; the mourning spirit comforted; and their trust in the promises of their Saviour renewed and strengthened.

A few officers, and other individuals from the upper classes of society, were observed among the emigrants; but the greater part were apparently peasantry and mechanics. The former had lost their commissions, on account of adherence to their religious principles.

Little efficient pecuniary aid could be rendered to the refugees by those who visited them; but that little was always received with the most affectionate and touching gratitude. Temporary awnings on the deck were the chief accommodation that the steam-boats could afford on their voyage from Hamburgh. The board of each party was supplied from one common purse; the poor (if possessing anything) had put their little all there, and the others contributed according to their means. Their fare and clothing were of the most homely description; three or four persons were sometimes observed partaking together from one common bowl of porridge. Their behaviour to each other was marked by a beautiful disinterestedness and generosity. Those who visited them were repeatedly informed that many individuals who had contributed largely to the common fund, preferred partaking of the fare of their companions, rather than that any marked difference should be observed.

Close inquiry was made whether anything like disaffection to their government could have led to the course they were pursuing; but this was always met by the most clear and satisfactory replies. On one occasion, when this question was directed to a group of young men, apparently peasants, their colour rose indignantly; and, with an unanimous burst of loyalty, they exclaimed, " Any one of us would lay down his life for our king."*

Are these the people to be driven from their Father-land, and compelled to seek a resting-

---

* Much interest has been felt in this country, respecting the kind treatment which six hundred of the Tyrolese Exiles have received from the King of Prussia; and it is right that this should be gratefully recognised; but surely his benevolent reception of a few hundred Austrian Protestants, is singularly inconsistent with the fierce persecution which for the last seven years has been carried on against thousands of his own loyal subjects, because they could not conscientiously unite with the New State Church. Having recently seceded from the Roman Catholic Communion, this was no hardship to the Zillerthalians.

place on foreign shores? If their own country disowns them, surely the hearts of British Christians will rise against such oppressive and cruel treatment; will regard them as " beloved for their fathers' sakes;" and seek, in some poor measure, to soften their sorrows, and wipe away their tears, and extend to them the hand of sympathy and love!

Even their oppressors cannot impugn their integrity, but are compelled to acknowledge their moral character unimpeachable. Various documents, respecting their sufferings and past history, have been received from Germany. These are too clear and circumstantial for any doubt to arise as to their veracity: they were printed on the continent, and have circulated there; and, as little or nothing has yet appeared in this country on the subject, it is believed that no better plan can be adopted for laying the case before the British public, than by the simple translation and publication of some of these pamphlets; a few of which, slightly abridged, are accordingly presented to the reader in this volume. Several of the Chapters consist of extracts from private letters, and other papers, kindly furnished by a gentleman interested in the cause. These could be backed by many others, were it well to increase the number of its pages; but a short and authentic account seemed preferable to one more extended.

May He who has all hearts in his own keeping, bless this feeble endeavour on behalf of a poor and afflicted remnant of his people, and turn a strong current of British love and sympathy towards them! Any pecuniary aid that may be advanced for assisting them, will be carefully appropriated to the most pressing wants of the parties concerned; either by forwarding it to those already in exile, or by applying it to the immediate use of such as are still likely to pass, from time to time, through this country.* This persecution continues; and by the latest accounts, many pious Lutheran pastors are still in prison. Should the Prussian government refuse to relax its coercive measures, some thousands of these worthy but oppressed people are intending to follow their friends, in the course of the coming year. Those who have already reached America, are in very straitened circumstances, and it is feared will have to pass through many severe trials before their settlement can be formed.

Several letters on these subjects have been received at Newcastle, from Pastor Grabau, since his short visit to that town. This excellent minister has been twice imprisoned, for six months; and was only released last spring, on account of apparently declining health.

Should their scanty means allow of doing so, it seems probable that the emigrants will eventually settle near Winsconsin, in the neighbourhood of

* Contributions will be thankfully received by Barnett, Hoare, and Co., Bankers, London, or by the Union Joint Stock Bank, Newcastle-upon-Tyne, on behalf of the Committee appointed in Newcastle, for the relief of the Lutheran emigrants.

Lake Michigan; but many left home almost pennyless, and their common fund has been severely drained by the unavoidable expenses of their long voyage and journey.

They rejoice, notwithstanding, at their deliverance from religious bondage. They can freely serve and worship their God; and having nobly maintained their integrity, are permitted to rely with filial confidence on his promises, that, according to Romans viii. 35, 39, neither tribulation, nor persecution, nor famine, nor nakedness, nor peril, nor any other distress, shall be able to separate them from his love in Christ Jesus.

Newcastle-on Tyne,
    12*th Mo.* 26*th*, 1839.　　　　　A. H. R.

CHAPTER I.

BRIEF OUTLINE OF THE PERSECUTION, BY PASTOR GRABAU.

Extract from a Letter, dated Liverpool, August 9th, 1839, from John Andrew Augustus Grabau, Pastor to the Prussian Emigrants, who lately crossed the North of England, on their way to America.

It is your wish that I should give you an account of the persecution we have endured in Prussia, which I will briefly do, as God shall enable me.

In the year 1817, when I was still but a youth, the Lutheran church celebrated the Third Centenary of the Reformation, on which occasion the King of Prussia sought to effect an union with the Reformed Church. However, it was not until 1830, that the Lutherans clearly understood the nature of this union. But on the occasion of the celebration of the festival of the presentation of the Augsburg Confession in that year, the King of Prussia gave orders that a new liturgy should be introduced into the Lutheran church in his dominions, respecting which he asserted, that it was in conformity with, and according to the Augsburg Confession. Many of the Lutheran clergy hesitated to accept of this liturgy; but were by degrees induced to do so, by the artifices and violence of the civil authorities.

It was a Lutheran church in Breslau, which first openly refused to accept the liturgy; and proved, by printed statements in their defence, that this liturgy rendered void the Lutheran Confession. Light upon this point extended itself, from Breslau over all the Prussian dominions; and in 1834 and 1835, when I was minister at Erfurt, in Prussian Thuringia, I also began to see the subject in a clearer point of view.

In the latter year, about nineteen ministers had publicly renounced the new form of worship, from conscientious motives; on which account they were either dismissed or imprisoned by the civil authorities. The congregations, following, for the most part, the example of their preachers, were also fined and imprisoned; when, for instance, they refused to have their children baptized according to the new formula; or if they did not attend the new form of worship, and held Lutheran divine service by themselves, according to the ancient apostolic mode. But the heavier the pressure and the longer it lasted, the more clearly did Lutheran Christians perceive the real nature of the Prussian Religious Union.

In a few years, about twenty-thousand publicly renounced the New United Church, and declared that they would abide by their ancient apostolic (Lutheran) church. They frequently presented petitions for toleration, to the king and his ministers, but in vain. They proved that their confession was rendered void by the new form of worship, but received no other answer than that it was not true; that they might still believe what they pleased; but must belong to the United Church.

The Lutherans, however, declared that they could not do so, as long as the latter did not confess the Lutheran religion, in its form of worship; they also requested to have their ministers set at liberty. But these requests were in vain. Their distress continuing to increase, and the Lutherans seeing the spiritual danger to which they were exposed by it, resolved to emigrate.

The Rev. A. Kavel was the first, who, on leaving Prussia, went to England; his congregation removed with him to Australia. The Rev. Mr. Krause was the next. He proceeded to Buffalo, in North America, with a single deputy. His congregation accompany me. The Rev. Otto Wehran was the third who left Prussia, and emigrated to France with his family. I am now the fourth, and am proceeding with about a thousand Lutheran Christians, on board five vessels, from Liverpool to New York.

On the 10th of June, I left the prison at Heiligenstadt, in the Prussian province of Eichsfeld, by way of Magdeburg to Hamburgh, accompanied by a gens d'arme. Since the 1st of March, 1837, I have spent above eight months in prison; then ten months as a fugitive, pursued day and night by gens d'armes; and then again nine months in prison. During the last month, my imprisonment was rendered in some measure more tolerable, in consequence of my illness.

Last March, the congregation who are now emigrating, wished that I would accompany them, which, through the Divine assistance, I am now enabled to do. We hope to find the Rev. F. E. Krause in Buffalo, and shall request him to remove to the place where we intend to settle, in order that our congregation may have the services of two ministers. The Silesian brethren, who accompany us, belonged originally to the flock of Mr. Krause, who is now in Buffalo; but the two congregations will in future (D. V.) constitute one; since it is our intention to gather together the fugitive church in North America. May the most merciful God assist us in effecting this!

Several ministers in Prussia are either still in prison, wandering about as fugitives, or banished to distant places. Their congregations observe their ancient mode of worship, without ministers. The elders in such cases read a sermon.

Translated from the German, by Samuel Jackson.

A pleasing memoir of Pastor Grabau appeared shortly after his visit to Hamburgh, in the "Lutheran Pilgrim," a weekly periodical published in that city. The writer speaks highly of the uprightness of his character, of his patience, humility, and unwearied perseverance. He remarks that his conversation overflowed with a fervent love to God and man; and that his public addresses, though not eloquent, were clear and forcible, and showed a constant earnestness to draw the minds of his hearers to their Saviour.   ED.

CHAPTER II.

FURTHER PARTICULARS, BY C. B. SCHULTHES.

Extracts from a similar account, signed by Carl Benjamin Schulthes, Elder of a Congregation in the Circle of Militsch, Silesia, dated Hamburgh, April 23d, 1839.

After service was over, our dear pastor (Mr. Krause) was seized by two sergeants of the police, and the names of the members of the community were taken down, in order that they might be fined or committed to prison.

Our revered pastor was imprisoned for one year and eight days in Militsch, and was afterwards carried forcibly away to the fortress of Erfurt, where he remained three quarters of a year, in addition to the imprisonment at Militsch; and very probably he would be there at this very moment, if he had not found an opportunity to take flight, in order to serve his community. He was pursued by means of the newspapers; but, through the mercy of God, was not caught.

During this time the persecutions grew more severe, and persons were fined twenty dollars for once attending Divine service. The poor were imprisoned, and those who had some property were distrained upon, to the amount of three or four times the fine levied. Some were even deprived of their most necessary garments, which were taken from their bodies and sold. Mechanics and workmen were obliged to deliver up their tools. Divine service was sometimes disturbed, and those who attended it were forcibly driven out of the house. A poor woman was prematurely delivered, and died in consequence of this ill-treatment.

If a child had been baptized by a Lutheran minister, the father or god-parents were forced to name the same; and if they refused to do so, to avoid betraying him, they were obliged to pay treble the sum of the costs, for the benefit of the minister of the United Church. Some children were taken away from their parents, and were baptized a second time by the United Minister; and upon reaching fourteen years of age, if they could not produce a certificate to prove that they had been confirmed by a Minister of the United Church, the parents were compelled to pay five dollars a month for the attendance of such children at the public schools; or, if they could not do this, were imprisoned.

All our representations to the government were useless; and we were often told, that we were treated far too mildly; we ought to have been beheaded, because we were rebels who opposed the king.

One of the elders, named Hubsch, was imprisoned with a common thief. He was left four days without food, (and if the thief had not shared his own with him, he might have been starved,) contrary to the law of the land, which ordains that whoever leaves a prisoner three days without food shall be deprived of his office. Mr. Hubsch had been four days without food; and when he complained to the government he remained without any answer, because he was a Lutheran; who is worse than a highwayman or murderer, as the magistrates have several times repeated!

Another of the elders, named Sattler, having several times been observed to attend Divine service, had a horse, cow, and thirteen hogs taken from him, which amounted to seventy-nine dollars; and, besides this, he was imprisoned for nine weeks. This man had been an officer in the army, and had obtained the iron cross, which is a sufficient proof that he was no bad subject.

I might tell you many more such things, if I did not fear to tire your patience. What I have said will be sufficient to show you, that we do not seek comfortable days. No! if they had but granted us some favours; if we might have been allowed to have our Sunday service in our own houses, and to receive the holy sacraments from our own ministers, we should willingly have borne every oppression. But all this was refused; wherefore we have undertaken this emigration, trusting in the Almighty Lord, who has promised to be with us.

On the 3d of January, when our brethren left Breslau, they were driven out by the police, and have left their country like delinquents; though they lived there as faithful subjects. May the Lord our God have mercy upon our enemies, and change their hearts!

CHAPTER III.

EXTRACTS FROM THE APPEAL OF PASTOR KAVEL.

The following additional information, quoted from the appeal of an excellent Lutheran Pastor, is dated as far back as the year 1836, and is corroborative of the foregoing extracts.

In 1822, there appeared a new Liturgy, destined, in the first instance, for the royal chapel, at Berlin, as expressed in its title. It was introduced by degrees into other churches, towns, and villages; a part of the clergy already in office accepting it voluntarily, whilst all those that were to be appointed, were under the necessity of subscribing to it, or else did not obtain preferment. The reception of the new Liturgy was afterwards urged throughout the kingdom. Considerable opposition was raised, and much was written against it. Amongst others who opposed its reception, was the celebrated Schleiermacher. The magistracy of Berlin rejected it, and also twelve clergymen of that city. To induce the dissentients to receive the Liturgy, and in order to meet the various objections, a new edition was prepared, in the second part of which, many of the old prayers and formularies were inserted; which decided the majority of the clergy, amongst whom were the twelve above-mentioned, to receive it.

The year 1830 now approached, on the 25th of June in which, the third centenary of the presenting of the Augsburg Confession was celebrated. It was desired that on that day the new Liturgy should be read in all the churches. But as some of the Lutheran clergy, among whom was Dr. Scheibel, Professor in Breslau, could not conscientiously agree to this, he was suspended from his office, against the will and to the great grief of his flock. The same fate, the year following, befel all the preachers who did not receive the new Liturgy, or who had laid it aside again, after being convinced of their error. They were dismissed from their office; and if they ventured to preach the gospel and administer the sacraments in private houses to their forsaken parishioners, according to the Lutheran formula, which has been in use for the last three hundred years, they were thrown into prison, and compelled with their families to quit their respective parishes. And those Lutheran families, who, from fidelity to their church and Confession, took no part in the public worship of the established church, but mutually edified each other in private houses, were, also, either fined or imprisoned. These persecutions have been the most violent in Silesia and the grand-duchy of Posen, where most of the inhabitants are Lutherans. Some of the Lutheran preachers are still in prison; others wander about the country, with great difficulty and danger, to minister the word of God and the sacraments, during the night, in remote places, in order not to be disturbed by the police. For since the edict of 1834, prohibiting any meetings of Christians for mutual edification, unless by express permission of the Consistories (which, having subscribed to the Union, do not grant such permission to those Lutherans who have not adopted it)—all Lutheran divine service is rendered illegal.

There are thousands of Lutherans who live in this persecuted state. And why are they punished? Not for resisting the civil powers appointed by God, nor for refusing obedience to the laws of society; for they give unto Cæsar the things that are Cæsar's; but solely because they cannot receive the new Liturgy. Our opponents indeed, say, " You may adopt the Liturgy without joining the Union;" but who can do this, since the former has merely the latter for its object? * Gladly

---

* Already, in 1830, have *two Counsellors of the United Church*, Drs. Schulz and Von Cöln, in their treatise " concerning theological liberty," demonstrated that none of the Lutheran and reformed written Confessions, have been able to preserve their established principles in the United Church.

One of these distinguished Professors remarks as follows, "The United Evangelical Church has not, as yet, any common valid written Confession to show. And this Union cannot duly consist with the confession heretofore proceeding from the separate churches. Should each Evangelical Church continue in its distinct Confession, then cannot both these diverse and contradictory, yet mingled congregations, be any more considered ecclesiastically, as one united congregation."

"*Short Extract from the Concordia.*"   J. L. F.

would we unite, if it were only a real union; for we Lutherans, also, long that there may be one fold and one shepherd.

But we cannot regard that as a holy christian church, which persecutes another church. This is the case with the new United Church of Prussia, which tolerates neither those that are strictly Lutheran, nor such as are strictly reformed. He that does not adopt the new Liturgy, whether he be Lutheran or reformed, is persecuted.

Hence, he who belongs to the United Church, must at the same time, either actively or passively, consent to the persecution and suppression of the Lutheran and reformed churches as they have existed for three centuries. But we Lutherans, feel it to be contrary to conscience to belong to a church which persecutes Christian brethren; and on this account, were there no other motive, could not have communion with it. Who are we, that we should judge our brethren? Every one must stand or fall to his own master. We wish not to hinder any one from joining the United Church: we merely beg for toleration for ourselves. (Signed)

AUGUSTUS KAVEL,

Pastor of the Lutheran Church, at Klemzig, near Zullichau, on the borders of Silesia.

CHAPTER IV.

SEIZURE OF THE LUTHERAN CHURCH AT KAULWITZ.

The following Account is extracted from a Periodical work, printed at Leipsic, in the year 1835, and may be taken as a specimen of the forcible seizure of the Lutheran churches, by the Commissioners of the Prussian Government.

On the morning of September 12th, 1834, forcible possession was taken of the Lutheran church at Kaulwitz, by the Commissioners of government, who arrived there on that day with two policemen. They were received with loud lamentations and weeping from the women, who, with other parishioners, had collected round the church and parsonage. Pastor Biehler was thus interrogated by the superintendant, " Will you accept the New Agenda with the modifications adapted for this province?" His answer was " No." He was again asked and admonished, but again replied in the negative. Upon which refusal, the superintendant pronounced his suspension. A protocol was drawn out, and the Pastor was required to deliver up the keys of the church. He referred them to the community, who then unitedly declared, that they could not conscientiously do this. The keys were at length taken by force from the churchwarden; but on trying the doors it was found that some of the women had stopped the key-holes with wax, thinking that this was the best way of guarding their beloved church.

After several men had returned in succession, without having been able to effect an entrance, the Counsellor of the Province went in person to try his skill, but could not succeed. Thus baffled in their attempts, the offer of a drunken tax-gatherer was accepted, who proposed to break a window and climb through it. He did so, and was followed by several others, who thus managed to open the door from within. The Pastor was then compelled to repair to the building, and make a surrender of the church books, and vessels from the sacristy.

Though deeply tried he was supported, and endeavoured to comfort his weeping flock. Full possession having at length been taken, and the books and seals secured, the Commissioners departed.

"*Neues und Altes für Lutheraner.*"

J. D. L.

CHAPTER V.

OUTRAGE UPON THE CHURCH AT HÖNIGERN, AND BARBAROUS TREATMENT OF THE CONGREGATION.

On Tuesday, at 12 o'clock at noon, a body of troops, consisting of four hundred infantry, thirty cuirassiers, and fifty hussars, advanced upon Hönigern, in Mikovski, (Silesia,) from their quarters, about a mile from that place. They were well received, and were astonished at finding a quiet, pious people; for they had been described to them as Polish rebels. Upon their march, when a short way from the church, the Major asked Weber Scholz, from Saabe, "Is it true, as they have written from Berlin, that the people stand before the church with pikes and pitch-forks?" "Oh, no!" was the answer, "only with their hymn-books!"

On the first day the soldiers were friendly; and, in order that the people might not collect on the day following before the church, a report was spread that the military were merely passing through on their route to Poland; the baggage waggons were also ordered to be loaded early on Wednesday morning.

At half-past four A. M. the next day, the whole of the troops marched up to Hönigern. Then the infantry surrounded the church on all sides; the hussars posted themselves on the east, the cuirassiers on the west; and thus the 200 members of the community, who had watched their beloved church through the whole snowy winter night, were hemmed in. The cavalry blocked up the approaches, and drove away those that came near.

The President and the commanding Major then summoned them to leave the church, reminded them of the obedience due to the King, and warned them of the consequences of refusal. Reply was made, "We stand here in defence of our faith, and ecclesiastical freedom." *Answer:* "We leave you your faith." *A Voice:* "But not the undisturbed confession of it." The Major then gave them five minutes for consideration. The congregation sung. The Major summoned them again, and gave another five minutes. They continued to sing. He then summoned them for the third time, and ordered the soldiers to load their guns. Here a gun went off. The ball passed through the second window from the altar, and struck the northern side of the building. The hedges round the church were then broken down. The soldiers advanced in close ranks, and pushed away the people, and with the butt ends of their guns broke open the door and rushed in. This deed was done early in the morning, while it was yet dark.

The people fled without so much as raising a finger in opposition, and dispersed on all sides: but how were they terrified when they found they were not allowed to go home in peace; the cavalry turning upon them, and striking them with the flat sides of their swords—many of the blades breaking with the violence of the strokes! Some of the broken pieces are still preserved.

Several of the women received severe blows; the names of these are Schulz, Muller, &c. (others given in the original.) A child of twelve years, and an aged person of seventy, are mentioned among the sufferers. The first-named woman lost much blood from a cut in the head, so that it flowed through her straw bonnet. This happened at a distance from the church. Many fled, and took refuge in houses; but they were dragged from thence by the soldiers, one by the hair of his head; the police crying out, at the same time, " The name of the King must be respected ! " One woman was dragged from a stable, and beat so unmercifully, that she was confined to her bed for several days. Two other persons were rode down by the horses; and another was struck so severely, that he fell down senseless.

Eight persons were taken up and imprisoned; one named Charlotte Schlemmel, for saying, " If our beloved King, for whom we have prayed so often, could see how ill we are treated, his heart would bleed." Some other inconsiderate words escaped the sufferers; for instance, one who had formerly been a soldier, and whose wife had been severely beat, till she bled, exclaimed, " I would know how to finish those gallant cuirassiers." This man was handcuffed and taken to prison. The attack lasted for two hours.

The Major and his Adjutant quartered themselves in the pastor's house. The pastor's wife had left home three weeks previously, to attend her sick husband at Breslau. The soldiers broke open the pantry, store-rooms, and wardrobes, and helped themselves freely: this, however, was afterwards inquired into, and the proprietor indemnified.

The first day, the quartering of the soldiers upon the inhabitants, was general and equal, except that eight individuals, who had joined the State Church, received none; but on the Wednesday, the most faithful of the Lutherans were burdened with the greatest number of soldiers. The deputy Hillman, who had been beat, carried to prison, and deprived of an ox, received fifteen men; the deputies—Litze, Berger, and Tabitz, twelve hussars; and Klunz, twenty of the infantry.

On Christmas-day there was church parade. The soldiers were ordered to provide themselves with their military hymn-books and cartridges. Hahn, the Counsellor of the Consistory, the Superintendant Kelsch, and Pastor Bauch, stood by the altar. The Superintendant handed to the latter the new agenda, or prayer-book. The Counsellor of the Consistory delivered an address from the altar; not on the birth of Christ; but to prove to the congregation that his christian sentiments coincided with those of their dismissed pastor. Pastor Bauch complained in his sermon, that the community showed little love to him, and spoke evil of him; and yet he was innocent of their misfortunes, and only obeying the royal commands. The few members present wept. Not that they were touched by the sermon, but from affliction at being compelled to listen to the voice of a stranger, instead of to that of their dearly beloved pastor. What had induced them to attend the service? Surely not free will; for the soldiers had been ordered to persuade some one from every house to visit the church. A sergeant who was quartered with twelve men in the house of Wenzel, a peasant at Eckersdorf, said to him, "Dear host, go yourself, or send some one to church, otherwise you will have to pay dearly for it; for we do not march until there is order re-established in the attendance at church." The country being a poor one, and this a year of unusual scarcity, the quartering was a pressing burden to the people.

The President went from place to place, accompanied by the Counsellor of the Consistory and the Counsellor of the Province, and declared " The introduction of the New Agenda, is the will and command of the King, and you are disobedient and refractory if you do not go to church." It was continually laid before the people, that till they did this they would not get rid of the soldiers. The Counsellor of the Consistory constantly assured them, that, though the New Agenda was to be used in the church, yet they might remain Lutherans as before, and receive baptism and the Lord's-supper, according to the old Lutheran forms, and that the sermon also might be Lutheran. But all these were but verbal assurances. No one can be surprised that with such persuasions, and under the heavy burdens occasioned by the quartering, most of those who had previously stood firm to the church of their fathers, and to their beloved pastor, went to church, some on the second festival, and others on the Sunday following the festival.

Those who were frightened—to whom the most incredible things had become a sad reality, saw that attendance at the church was the only means of preventing these military devouring the whole of their scanty provisions. The following words were used to Squire Fogdt: "You are a perjured man; for as a vassal, you have sworn obedience to the King, and you are for the Old Agenda, though you are aware that the will of his Majesty is decisive for the New one." The landlords were at length induced to go to church on the Sunday following the festival, and on Monday the military marched off, after a stay of six days.

If they had not been instructed to compel the people to go to church by quartering the soldiers upon them, orders would have been given for their removal after the capture of the building. At the present time, only a few individuals attend the service there, and fewer still receive the Lord's-supper. A still smaller number would do so, if a report had not been spread, that those who did not visit the church, would have to pay the fifteen hundred dollars previously imposed on them. In addition to this, policemen have been stationed at Hönigern, to prevent those visits by which one might strengthen another in his faith. Under all these circumstances, but few stand firm; none, indeed, but those who, as Bible Christians, enlightened by the Spirit of God, have looked through the State Agenda and State Union, and would rather suffer the loss of all their property, than become members of such a church.

Neues und Altes für Lutheraner.
J. D. L.

Printed at Leipsic,
1835.

CHAPTER VI.

VEXATIOUS PROCEEDINGS AGAINST BARON VON KOSZUTSKI.

Taken from "Die neueste Geschichte der Lutherischen Kirche," published at Altona, 1836.

The following Narrative will serve to show the vexatious proceedings adopted against a prominent individual, who, after the neighbouring churches had been closed against the Lutheran worship, opened his own house for devotional purposes.

Baron Von Koszutski, proprietor of the estates of Great Tschunkawe and Schwiebedawe, is a young nobleman, who has proved himself a faithful witness to the truth; first, by the bold and open confession of his faith, and since, by the unwavering fidelity and patience with which he has cheerfully submitted to imprisonment, and great loss of worldly substance.

Ten years ago, he travelled, in company with Pastor Kellner, through several countries of Europe, and, through his instrumentality, was brought to a saving knowledge of the truth, so that, being actuated by the most heartfelt conviction, he seceded from the Roman Catholic church, to which he had previously belonged, and united himself to the Lutheran, at a time when the flames of persecution were already kindled, and might be expected to blaze with still greater ardour. Death deprived him of his wife after they had been married but a short time, and, from that period, he occupied himself with the management of his estates, and the education of his infant daughter, with whom he lived in retirement. Family worship was regularly held in his house, and conducted by Gessner, then a candidate, and now pastor of the Lutheran community, in the circle of Lowenberg, where his labours have been greatly blessed. But the authorities were not long before they began to regard these proceedings with suspicious eyes; and, believing that the hated flame of Lutheranism was chiefly fanned by the presence of Gessner, his further residence with Baron von Koszutski was forbidden by the Council of the circle of Militsch.

Pastor Krause was afterwards invited by Von Koszutski, and domestic worship continued; but the police were sent as spies, and, in many instances, disturbed the proceedings. In February, 1835, Von Koszutski was fined ten dollars; then again, for worship held in his house on the 8th of March, twenty dollars.

Pastor Biehler, having been invited to Kaulwitz, went thither, and, on the 20th of March, administered the Lord's-supper to thirty-one communicants. This religious festival was discovered; and the fines levied upon Von Koszutski in consequence, amounted to sixty dollars, and the others present were fined the same sum. A policeman was quartered in Pastor Biehler's house to keep constant guard over him; and as the government considered Von Koszutski to be the main support of the Lutherans in that district, their attention was naturally directed toward him.

A certain part of the castle at Great Tschunkawe had been set apart for public worship, and service was performed in a regular manner according to the Wittenberg Agenda; sermons were also preached, and the Lord's-supper was administered. This was generally at a very early hour in the morning, or late at night, on account of the spies; yet the number attending these services was so great, that pastor Krause was, on some Sundays, occupied for eight hours successively. On the 6th of June, Pastor Krause received notice that he might expect to be severely fined if he persisted in conducting worship at Baron Von Koszutski's, and on Sunday, the 19th of July, he was accordingly arrested at the conclusion of the service, and taken as a prisoner to Militsch, where he was quartered at an hotel, under the guard of a patrole. Von Koszutski was then absent from Great Tschunkawe, having gone to Karlsbad, in Bohemia, for the re-establishment of his health. While there, he received a rescript from the Royal Government of Breslau, dated June 5th, which stipulated that he should no longer hold Lutheran church service in his house; and threatening him, in case he would not agree to this demand, with the loss of his liberty. If he would not promise to obey this order, a policeman was to be quartered upon him, at his expense, to watch his movements, and send back all who repaired thither for worship. In reply, Von Koszutski stated, that, conscientiously adhering to the word of God, he could not obey the government in this matter, but would submit to their impositions, in humble subjection to God's will. On July 25th, he returned to Great Tschunkawe; and on the following day (Sunday), just as service was concluded with his fellow believers, two policemen appeared from Militsch, and summoned Von Koszutski to follow them to town. He was in too weak a state to do so just then, but gave them his word of honour that he would appear before the Council on Monday, the 27th. Though expecting his physician that day, a policeman appeared, and he was obliged to follow him, and prepare for his imprisonment. All his rooms *were sealed up*, except two, one belonging to his little girl, the other to her governess,* and he was himself quartered at the hotel at Militsch, under the surveillance of a policeman, at his own expense.

Though Pastor Krause was quartered at the same house, he was not allowed to visit Von Koszutski; at most they were only permitted to

---

* The same measures were taken at Schwiebedawe, Von Koszutski's other estate, where, however, in compliance with the urgent request of the magistrate, his sitting room and a small room in the upper story, were left open for his daughter and her governess.

speak to each other if they met when walking, and that in the presence of their guards.

The expenses at the hotel amounted to an immense sum; for Pastor Krause alone, they came to a dollar a day. No one was admitted to visit them: they were, however, allowed to write, and both were cheered and comforted. Pastor Krause wrote on the 31st of July, "Praised be the Lord who has thought me worthy of suffering for him, and of losing my bodily liberty for his name's sake, that I might, through his grace, enjoy that liberty, wherewith Christ has made me free."

He wrote again, on the 8th of August; "Hitherto in his unbounded mercy, the Lord has so aided us, that all the cunning, flatteries, and threats of the enemy, have not only been prevented doing us injury, but have been of incalculable advantage in strengthening our faith. The Lord has given peace and joy to our souls, and we leave the termination of our sufferings to his pleasure, nor will we yield an hand's-breadth in any thing that concerns his honour. Blessed be the Lord through all eternity, for these proofs of his mercy."

Pastor Krause several times petitioned the government, to be allowed to remove to private lodgings; but at last received an answer from the Council, that he was to remain where he was. His guard was daily paid eighteen-pence on his account. On the 22d of August, a prosecution was opened against Pastor Krause, and the following order was read to him:—

"Pastor Krause shall be set at liberty, provided he promise to abstain from all worship, except such as is strictly private, and from the administration of every religious rite." Krause declared that on such conditions he could not accept the offered liberty, they being against his vow and conscience. He was then told he must return to prison. To his repeated petitions, that, to save expense, he might be allowed to take private lodgings, the Secretary of the circle gave him evasive answers, "that Von Koszutski would pay for them," &c. He was also reproached for having spoken to Koszutski, when they met during their walks.

On the 20th of September, Baron Von Koszutski's little daughter was permitted to visit the pastor. He was delighted to see her, this being the first visit he had received for two months. On the 2d of October he received an answer to two of his petitions to the following effect: "The Royal Upper Court of Justice, cannot interfere with the Royal Government, for Pastor Krause's liberation; seeing that he has not agreed to the indispensable conditions stipulated for the recovery of his liberty, viz. no more to attend illegal assemblies for public worship, and to abstain from acting in a sacerdotal capacity. He may therefore ascribe to himself his protracted imprisonment." Pastor Krause protested against the word "illegal," saying that he had never attended such assemblies, but merely Lutheran worship, allowed by the peace of Westphalia, as well as by the law of the land.* In the meantime, Von Koszutski was obliged to stay at the hotel from the day of his arrest, on the 27th of July. The shameful treatment and mortifications of all kinds which he experienced there, afford a striking example of the spirit with which the persecution has been carried on, and though Von Koszutski bore them with humility and resignation, his delicate state of health became confirmed under such treatment, and terminated in a serious illness. When he complained of the exorbitant demands of his landlord, the latter replied, that he had been empowered by the higher authorities, to ask from him three times more than he would have demanded from another person.† Von Koszutski was likewise required to pay the expenses of Pastor Krause, and his

---

* "After the Westphalian peace, the sovereign (being of the reformed confession in Lutheran countries), might regulate the court worship, and permit the free exercise of his confession, but could not change the established religion, laws, and ordinances of the church. The congregations had the right of electing their church-ministers, and school-masters, who, if a consistory (or, assembly of divines) of their religion, were near at hand, should be examined and ordained by it (or else by a special one, appointed by the congregations), and then undeniably ratified by the sovereign."

Geschichte der Lutherischen Gemeine in Breslau, 1832.   J. L. F.

† It was, however, afterwards discovered, that this was done by the suggestion of a person named Geise, a particularly active enemy of the Lutherans, and who spoke thus on his own responsibility.

guard. Some time after this, he was permitted to take private lodgings, but no one was allowed to visit him besides his little daughter Clara. Her governess was not allowed to accompany her. The fines levied upon him, on account of worship, amounted to three hundred dollars; but it was intimated to him, that he would immediately be set at liberty, if he would promise to hold no more religious assemblies. Truly, no small temptation! But Von Koszutski remained firm; and when he was, afterwards, again pressed to accept this offer, and even told that his fines would be remitted, and that he would be allowed to have family-worship,

none but his own household were present, and, also, that duty to his king called for this submission, Von Koszutski refused to accept his liberty on such terms, saying that it was his highest duty to obey the King of kings, and asking, how he could receive the sacrament without a church communion. In the mean-time, Von Koszutski did not neglect to petition the Royal Government at Breslau, for the redress of his grievances, according to legal forms. In the first of these petitions, dated the 4th of August, he says, "Must not the body as well as the mind suffer, under such treatment: I have a beloved child, my greatest joy on earth, whose education is dear to my heart; I am informed this child is not to visit me with her governess; what a prospect for the future! if there be no sympathy for the sufferings that are heaped upon a fellow-creature, for the purpose of making him deny his faith, perhaps, among those who read these lines, there will be a paternal heart that understands me—that will not deny the feelings of nature. I am, besides, the proprietor and manager of two extensive farms; no plans have been laid down for the future—I do not even know in what state the different branches of rural economy are, as I was not allowed time to review them. What will become of all these things? It has been asserted by the lower authorities, and spread among my tenants, that all such tenants and servants as hold my religious opinions, are likewise to be imprisoned. Obstinacy and disobedience have already been consequent on this report; for, knowing their landlord to be at a distance, they have no one to look up to. Should my lasting imprisonment be fixed on, for which the rude multitude wait with avidity, then all the bonds of order and discipline will be broken on my estate, and that, by the measures of those same authorities, who are instituted for the express purpose of maintaining good order. I would cheerfully suffer the spoiling of my worldly goods for conscience sake, as happened in the early stages of Christianity, and will happen in all subsequent persecutions; but must not acts of violence, committed under the show of right, shock the feelings of every just man? The law of our land honours conscience; and to compel men to violate it, is nothing less than to force them to commit moral suicide. The practice of Lutheran worship is, besides, confirmed by the treaty and peace of Westphalia: therefore, however ignorant government may appear to be of it, no pen can be used to dictate these persecutions, but conscience will whisper to the writer, "What thou doest is contrary to law."* But setting aside the earlier guarantees for religious liberty (which seem now to be mere formalities, in the most civilised state of Europe), how can the measures employed against me, be justified by the royal commands, which, indeed, prescribed fines for holding Lutheran church service, and in consonance with which edict, I have already been fined more than three hundred dollars, and the country will shortly behold the tragi-comic spectacle of the sale of my best cattle: but have the sealing up of my rooms and my imprisonment been also prescribed by the King? the imprisonment of an invalid—of a father—of a landed proprietor, who ought to see that order and discipline are maintained? It has been reported, that I am to be tried for rebellion; but I can only take this for idle talk, as a child

---

* "The Lutheran church has, for three hundred years, been in possession of rights in Silesia, which it owed to the peace of religion of 1555, confirmed by a letter of the Emperor Rudolph II. in the year 1609, through the Westphalian peace of 1648, and by the extension of the convention of Altranstadt of 1707, all of which, bestowed upon it the most extended privileges, which, besides, have been confirmed by Frederick the Great, by Wilhelm II. and the present king.—Our Lutheran church has still another foundation for its rights, in the general law of the land."

Extract from the letter signed by C. B. Schulthes.

may see that holding prohibited religious worship cannot be identified with such assemblies as meet to oppose themselves to the commands of government. But, if even such a prosecution were in store for me, my imprisonment would still be illegal, as my station in society is a sufficient surety for my non-withdrawal from the authorities. I should have imagined those authorities would have executed with reluctance the orders lately given them; yet they are not content without exceeding such orders. I will not speak here of justice and christian love; but my trust in mere humanity forbids me to believe, that the government can take pleasure in tormenting a fellow-creature without cause. Surely when His Majesty visits the province, it will be no joy to his heart to hear that the prisons in Silesia are filled with Christians, persecuted on account of their faith. The monarchs of Spain were shown such prisoners by the inquisitors, but our sovereign is no Spanish king of the times of the inquisition! I trust that the government, after conscientious and calm consideration of the above-mentioned reasons, will grant my humble request: viz., that I may be liberated from prison, and that an order may be given for my rooms to be unsealed; and I only add, that if this should not be done, my grief and bodily weakness may cause my death. But, by the blessing of God, I hope to be kept from committing any action against the dictates of my conscience. At any rate, I humbly request that the government will be graciously pleased to come to a speedy decision, and let me know my fate, if possible, within a week, there being the most urgent necessity for my release, or that, in case of liberty being still denied me, I may adopt my ulterior measures accordingly." To this petition the following answer was received, on the 11th of August, " In reply to your representation of the 4th inst. we can only say that we find, with deep regret, that the essence of your faith, and the dictates of your conscience, rest *in forms ;* by the observance or non-observance of which, you, and your fellow-sectarians, separate yourselves from the rest of evangelical Christians : for a doctrinal change has never been intended by the government; on the contrary, the state never wished to limit either your liberty of conscience, or that of any other individual. Domestic worship, therefore, in any form whatever, has never been prohibited. It may be seen then, that the conscience of each individual is free, but that the state will not tolerate assemblies which exceed the domestic circle, and that there is no violation of liberty of conscience, in the prohibition of such assemblies, as might be self-evident to you, and any impartial judge ; nay, in fact, to every one having the smallest idea of the constitution of a state. Because you have acted in contradiction to the prohibition of the authorities in holding public meetings—because you have expressly declared that you will not render obedience to the before-mentioned prohibition, nothing is left to us but to order your imprisonment, thus enforcing due obedience to the laws. We cannot fix upon the duration of your imprisonment, since that depends entirely on the Upper Court of Justice, to whom we have sent a copy of your representation. You may therefore address yourself to them. Your complaint about the prison expenses shall be further inquired into."

Breslau, 11th of August, 1835. Royal government division of the interior administration of clerical and scholastic affairs.

To the Baron Von Koszutski, of Great Tschunkawe.

Von Koszutski being referred to the Upper Court of Justice, addressed himself to it on the 19th of August. After the usual introduction, he added the following words, respecting the beforementioned rescript, dated Breslau, 11th of August. " Their rescript begins with calling me a *sectarian*; yet I have never been accused of deviating from the principles of the Lutheran church, since I became a member of it. I can only reply to this in the words of St. Paul, Acts xxiv. verses 5 & 14. " But this I confess unto thee, that after the way which they call heresy (sectarianism), so worship I the God of my fathers," &c. The government express their regret, that I do not look with their indifference on certain " forms," that is, articles of the church; which regret, I may observe, contrasts strangely with the cruel persecutions they have heaped upon me. I have surely deeper reason to regret that a Christian government can believe themselves called upon, in contradiction to the general law of the land, to treat a subject with such severity, on account of what they consider his error in religious matters. The authorities lay down this rule—that, provided domestic worship is permitted, no one has a right to complain of the limitation of liberty of conscience; but the sacraments of the Lord's-supper and baptism do not come within the compass of domestic worship, and are therefore not included in that liberty of conscience which the state allows. The command, Hebrews x. 24, 25, upon which christian worship all over the world is founded, is then to be annulled, and the rights of a religious society, confirmed by the treaty of Westphalia, Chap. 7, page 1, as well as by the assurances of all the monarchs of our royal dynasty, are to be superseded by that liberty of conscience which is granted by the royal government; and acting according to these treaties is incompatible with the well-being of the state! Besides, the royal government silently admit, that I have been deprived of my liberty, solely on account of having held worship according to my faith, and for having refused to stain my conscience in order to please men. They do not pretend that their proceedings are sanctioned, either by law or right, but order my imprisonment, solely because that was the only means by which they could accomplish their wishes. If the authorities were justified in acting thus, then I must consider myself indebted to them, for not having deprived me of my life, which would undoubtedly have been the surest way of preventing my exercising liberty of conscience. I am now, however, at the disposal of the Upper Court of Justice, from whom, I may hope for equitable treatment.

The Upper Court of Justice will see that no law sanctions my imprisonment, and the sealing up of my rooms. This unprecedented measure, is contrary to the dictates of humanity, and is a disgrace to the state in which it is put into operation. I therefore repeat my humble request for liberation from prison, and the unsealing of my rooms. How imperatively the state of my health calls for liberation, I beg leave to attest by the enclosed document from my physician. With due respect I subscribe myself, &c.

VON KOSZUTSKI."

After a delay of three weeks (although he had particularly requested a speedy answer), Von Koszutski received the following:—" Herewith you receive a copy of a rescript, sent to the royal government to-day, in reply to your petition of the 19th of August. We inform you, at the same time, that the government has twice desired, namely on the 14th and 30th of July that a prosecution should be opened against you for rebellion. We replied, on the 8th of August, that there was not a sufficient ground for such a proceeding toward you; even then, we requested the government to restore your liberty, provided there were no other grounds for the detention of your person. Having received, from the Silesian government, a copy of your petition, we repeated that request on the same day. We must therefore refer you to that court for your ulterior answer."

Breslau, September 3, 1835.
The Senate of the Silesian Upper Court of Justice.

In the mean-time, Von Koszutski had offered his best carriage and some cattle, for the payment of the so-called religious fines. They would not accept of these, but threatened him with putting an execution into his house, if he would not pay in cash. On the 2d of September, at 11, A. M. he received the following rescript from the County Court. "The Silesian government having fixed, by a decree of the 24th of August, the manner in which the fines are to be levied on your lordship (Ew. Hochwohlegeboren), I have ordered the bailiff, Steinmetz, to raise the two hundred and seventy dollars forfeited by you, for holding illegal religious meetings, by seizing, first the cash, and then other valuables, to make up the required amount.   Signed,   PRINCE HATZFELD."
Militsch, September 2, 1835.

Baron Von Koszutski immediately surrendered himself up to the court, where he met the Prince and Secretary, and addressed the former as follows: "Is it possible, your Highness, that the government can proceed in this manner, after having read my petitions?" The Prince replied, "It is expressly commanded." *Von Koszutski,*

"But the law says, any one may give to the bailiff those things which can be best dispensed with, and of such are the goods that I propose to give." The Prince replied, " I adhere to the literal command;" whereupon Von Koszutski said, " If there be no longer in Prussia any law, which recognises the Lutherans, it is useless to say more."

When he came to his dwelling, he found the bailiff, accompanied by the commissioners, already at the door, and having requested them to enter, he desired the bailiff to read his instructions, which he did, but in an embarrassed manner, and with a faltering voice. In these instructions, the bailiff was ordered to seize the mortgages, then the bank-notes, and lastly the cash: but in the first instance to examine Von Koszutski's iron safe. On hearing this, Von Koszutski ordered his guard, and an officer named Steinwender, who happened to be present, to bring in his iron-safe from the next room, and gave up the key. Besides the papers contained in it, which were examined by Commissioner Neugebauer, there were six silver spoons, which Von Koszutski took out, and laid on his desk. To the question " Who is the owner of the sofa?" Von Koszutski answered " I am, as well as of the bed, looking-glass, and chairs;" and the bailiff then observed, that as no cash had been found, they must go and inform the Prince of it. This was done, and in ten minutes they returned with the answer; " It is his Highness's pleasure, that the writing-desk be examined." They found in the drawers of the desk, about thirty dollars; of these, he allowed the commissioner to take twenty-five, and the bailiff, seeing the money was nearly gone, begged he would likewise pay him for his trouble. Von Koszutski gave him the remainder, only reserving two dollars and a half for himself. All the other compartments were examined, but without finding any booty. When the bailiff told Von Koszutski, that it was the pleasure of his Highness, that he should give him a written declaration that he possessed neither mortgages, bank-notes, nor any other things of value, Von Koszutski replied, that he did not consider himself bound to send any answer to a verbal summons. The public sale of the goods distrained, took place on the 8th of September, and on the 15th of the same month, Von Koszutski received another rescript from the Silesian government, wherein he was once more offered his liberty on condition that he would enter into an engagement, to abstain from holding meetings for worship in his house. They also reprimanded him, for his obstinacy in refusing to pay the fines imposed for those he had already held, alleging that he had done so, in order that the sale of his goods by public auction, which had taken place in consequence of his contumacy, might *be published, and being read in foreign countries*, might injure the Prussian state. In reply to this offer from the government, Von Koszutski referred them again to Matt. x. 32, 33. Hebrews x. 25. and Acts v. 29.

At the same time the court required him to pay twenty dollars, as guard money for Pastor Krause. When Von Koszutski objected to this, the Counsellor replied, "Then we will place Pastor Krause in the county prison, where no watch is required." Von Koszutski then said, "If the lawful authorities demand that we shall pay the expenses of the guards provided for us, then I will cheerfully pay the money for myself and my friend." The Counsellor replied, "The government left to our discretion, the measures to be taken with you; the watch money amounts, altogether, to thirty-six dollars; and, if this be not paid, you may expect the bailiff to make another call upon you, three days hence." Shortly after Von Koszutski received the following rescript from the royal government:—

"The Upper Court of Justice have informed us, that you have repeatedly petitioned them for your release, and the unsealing of your rooms; the first petition being founded upon the certificate of your physician, which, however, contains nothing except the general principle, that exercise in the open air is better than imprisonment in a room, applied to your particular case. We are the less disposed to set you at liberty, as it depends on *yourself* to obtain it, having only to declare your obedience to the royal commands: viz. to frequent no conventicles, and to admit no strangers to your domestic worship. If you agree to these stipulations, the local authorities have the power to release you, and to unseal your rooms."

Breslau, September 13, 1835.
Division of the interior for the administration of clerical and scholastic affairs.

On the 18th of September, Von Koszutski again addressed himself to the Silesian government, to whom he had been referred by the Upper Court of Justice, begging them to set him at liberty according to the rescripts of that court, dated respectively, 8th and 15th of August, and 3rd of September, and that this liberty might be unconditionally granted, and not clogged with any restrictions to which his conscience would not allow him to submit, for he observes, "In the government rescript, dated the 3d of September, it is said that I am only required to promise not to visit any conventicles. This surprised me greatly, as I have never been accustomed to frequent conventicles, nor have I expressed any wish to do so. The second condition which the government prescribes, is, that I do not admit strangers to my domestic worship. Were I to be allowed to present any petition in person to my earthly lord and king, I should not have the power of preventing any other equally privileged individual from accompanying me to the royal presence. Much less, dare I then, refuse to allow others to invoke, in fellowship with me, the mercy of the King of kings, and Lord of lords! For acting thus, in direct opposition to the Divine command, my prayers might be turned into a curse. If the government prevent my doing so, they will have to answer for it to the great Judge of all; but for myself, I shall adhere to the word of the Lord, recorded in Acts v. 29. "We ought to obey God rather than men." In conclusion, I once more entreat the government, to give me, as soon as possible, unconditional freedom. Should my humble request meet again with a refusal, all that is left me will be, by appealing to the highest authorities, to make a last attempt for my restoraration to social intercourse."

To this, Von Koszutski received the following answer: "The wording of your latest petition for dismissal from prison, dated the 18th of the present month, plainly shows your slight respect for the law, and want of obedience to the state and its legal authorities. The real cause of your imprisonment is, your refusal to prevent strangers attending your domestic worship; and the prolongation of it, you may, therefore, ascribe to your own contumacious resistance to the government's requisitions. In reference to your observations, respecting the decrees of the Senate of the Upper Court of Justice, of the 8th and 15th of August, and the 3d of September, we would inform you, that when the rescript of the 15th of August was sent off, we were ignorant of the Senate's refusal to open an action against you for rebellion, and, therefore, referred your petition to them. They certainly ordered you to be set at liberty, but, only, in case there were no other accusation against you to warrant your detention. You are now turned over to the care of the police, whose duty compels them to enforce the laws. And, since the usual means, persuasions, warnings, and fines, have been of no effect, nothing remains but to limit your personal liberty. You must give up the practice of holding and attending conventicles; such assemblies being prohibited. And if you will but reflect for a moment, that we are not appointed to judge about the propriety of laws, but to obey them, and see that others do the same—you will perceive a justification of our seeming severity; since, however disagreeable it may be to us, on the one hand, to use such severity—we feel ourselves called upon, on the other, to prevent the disturbance of quietness and public order, by proceedings carried on under the cloak of religion.

It is, then, our firm resolve, to procure obedience to the law, and in cases of necessity, to use for that purpose the severest measures in our power. Nor will our resolution be shaken, by the most wanton obstinacy, and guilty disobedience on your part. The way stands open to you, as to every one else, to appeal against our proceedings:—but we do not yet despair of seeing you close your ears to the insinuations of self-sufficiency, and deluded enthusiasm,* and listening to the voice of law and civil order, relinquish those illegal practices, by which

---

* Obedience to the commands of God, is then termed, by the government of Breslau "wanton obstinacy," "guilty disobedience," and "deluded enthusiasm."

Dr. J. G. Scheibel.

you set so bad an example, and produce consequences, that you will surely repent, when the dark cloud shall have left your eyes, and truth, in all her brightness, stands before you. We need not add more, as you know how to act, in order to effect your liberation."

Breslau, September 26, 1835.

On the 29th of September, Von Koszutski received the following rescript from the Council of the County. "If the prison expenses be not paid, within three days, Pastor Krause will be put, without further notice, into the county gaol."

Von Koszutski was not the only sufferer from the persecution; the greater part of the community at Great Tschunkawe have been thrown into the furnace of affliction, on account of their faith; but they, like him, have been enabled to make a good confession.*

Many of these people are poor; and the few pigs they had fed, for their winter's sustenance, have been taken from them, and sold; and, as the money obtained in this way, does not cover the fines, they expect a second distraint. Notwithstanding these trials, they are yet of good cheer in the Lord, and the persecuted Lutheran church is daily receiving new members.

At Great Tschunkawe, Schwiebedawe, Militsch,

---

* A private letter from Germany, in the year 1838, confirms the correctness of the above statement, and speaks of Baron Von Koszutski as desiring to emigrate. He remained in confinement for "some months."

and some other villages, severe punishments and fines have been inflicted. Sattler, from Guhre, a loyal officer, knight of the iron cross,* and also knight of the cross of Christ, was put into the county gaol, for having held Lutheran worship, and was fined eighty dollars; which fine was to be repeated, each time he committed the same offence. When in prison, they tried to make him retract, proposing to set him free, and remit the fine, if he would promise to hold Lutheran worship no more. They invited Sattler (who is an elder) to accept liberty on these terms, and told him he might return to prison again, if he found himself unable to fulfil them. This otherwise firm man, allowed himself to be over-persuaded, and accepted this condition of liberty on the 26th of August; but he found neither comfort at home, nor joy in prayer. The Lord gave him a great support in his truly Christian wife, who, with his children, was distressed that he had accepted liberty on such terms; and his conscience becoming burdened by the thought, that as an elder, he, at least, ought to have remained firm to his confession, after a few days he was induced to revoke his promise, and voluntarily return to prison, and allow the distraint to proceed.

* See "Extracts from the letter, signed by C. B. Schulthes." There is a slight difference in the list of goods distrained, but no one can be surprised at such an accidental discrepancy; C. B. S.'s address having been hastily written, at Hamburgh, more than three years after the period referred to.—EDITOR.

He and his family have since recovered their former cheerfulness; and when, on the 15th of September, the Court again invited him to return home, on the same conditions as before—at least for the day when the bailiff was to distrain the goods—he firmly refused. On the 16th of September, the distraint was effected; and for the eighty dollars fine, the bailiff took ten pigs, two capital milch cows, and a horse, which the bailiff valued, altogether, at seventy-nine dollars and three-quarters. On *Sunday*, the 20th, the cattle were publicly sold at Guhre.

In Great Tschunkawe, the fines of ten individuals, for having attended Lutheran worship, amounted to two hundred and fifty dollars. One female paid her fine in cash, but from the rest, they took away pigs, geese, leather, shoes and boots, earthenware, clocks and watches.

At the public worship held in the beginning of September, the police took down the names of two hundred and forty persons, who were fined two dollars each.

In September, the fines already amounted to fourteen hundred dollars; which even Prince Hatzfeld, assured Baron Von Koszutski, would be remitted if he would promise to abstain from holding Lutheran worship. A poor old man, named Zoller, from Suhlau, was fined four dollars, for having, with his son, a youth of sixteen years of age, attended Lutheran worship; and being too poor to pay this fine, and nothing equivalent being found in his dwelling, they were both sent, on the

Sabbath evening, to Militsch, where they were thrown into a dreary dungeon, and kept behind iron gates, secured with heavy locks, the son for two, the father for three days. On the 22d of September, as his Majesty was returning from Kalrsch, he passed through Militsch, and several petitions were handed to him, for the release of the pastors and their imprisoned fellow-believers; and for the undisturbed performance of Lutheran church service; but no answer to these petitions, has yet been received.   J. D. L.

CHAPTER VII.

HISTORY OF THE PERSECUTION OF THE LUTHERAN CHURCH IN PRUSSIA, SINCE THE YEAR 1830, BY M. ERNST. (PRINTED 1837.) *

THE Lutheran church in Prussia, which for conscience sake remains faithful to its old Confession of faith, guaranteed by treaties of peace, and the coronation oaths of our sovereigns, is fiercely persecuted by the state and police church—(polizeikirche.) A history of the same, particularly relating to its severity in Silesia, was published in Alsace two years ago, when the whole edition was quickly and eagerly bought up. The persecutions have not ceased since that time, but still continue, and become from day to day more cruel and terrible. We have lately received intelligence from trust-worthy men, which we communicate to our readers in their own words.

I.

Mr. Krause, pastor of the Lutheran community in the circles of Militsch, Trebnitz, and Wartenberg in Silesia, was seized and imprisoned at Militsch, because in obedience to the word of God, and his official oath, he had rejected the

---

* This document though important, may be considered desultory, a defect which is accounted for in the concluding remarks.—ED.

command of the United church to resign his office as Lutheran pastor. By the arbitrary decree of the State church (not by legal judgment) he was confined for more than a year, and forty-two weeks of that time in a narrow prison. His congregation in the mean time went on increasing, for honest minds were convinced by those dark deeds of their anti-christian principle, and openly acknowledged this before the magistrates. Notwithstanding the separation from their pastor, they maintained public worship through their superintendants, and would not be deterred from it, either by the police, or by weekly judicial examinations, or by threatened fines and imprisonments. The superintendants of the different communities when deprived of their pastors, some of whom have been banished and others imprisoned, do not preach themselves in religious assemblies, but according to their pastors' advice, read each time a sermon from a book, and before and after it a prayer from the old Wittenberg church prayer book.

The Lutherans in Prussia would feel thankful, if assemblies of twenty or fifteen, or even ten persons were allowed to meet together; they would then divide themselves and perform worship in their different houses, but the assembling of even a few individuals for this purpose is not allowed.

If the ever-spying police find merely two or three neighbours, who have met for the purpose of reading a sermon, or a chapter from the Bible, they are seized—deprived of their property, and then imprisoned and punished as rebels. Through the kind Providence of God, some of the travelling ministers have not yet fallen into the hands of their persecutors, and these have been still enabled to administer the sacrament to the congregations.

In order to accomplish the purpose of destroying the Lutheran church (guaranteed by the oaths of kings, and other privileges for these three hundred years) the State church imprisoned several members of Mr. Krause's congregation for days, months, and quarters—distrained from one of the wealthiest among them 1160 francs, from another 320—took from the poor their clothing, cattle, house utensils, and even the vessels in which they prepared their food, extorting altogether 5200 francs from this poor community, in addition to which, they threatened, ill-treated, beat them, and used all the arts of cunning and arbitrary force to disperse them. But the people remained firm, and cheerfully suffered the ill-treatment and loss of their property.

The State church expected to dissolve the community by removing their pastor from them, but they were mistaken. It not only remained unshaken, but increased during the imprisonment of their father (minister) one hundred souls.

This unjust imprisonment of Pastor Krause convinced the people of the tyranny of the State church, more than a volume of sermons could have done. This community has also extended locally. It now includes a space of 32 square miles (equal to 144 English).

The State church having deprived the Lutherans of their public places of worship, now sought to disturb their private religious meetings. The people then retired into the woods to worship; the children were also taken there to be baptized. Spies are engaged in all places, (particularly in Silesia) whose vigilance is excited by the promise of premiums, so that the holy sacrament can only be administered during the nights, for all the village and town magistrates are charged to have every Lutheran pastor arrested wherever he may found. Nevertheless the Lutheran church increases every where, for the most simple and unlearned must perceive that that cannot be the right church which practises such barbarous cruelties against those who differ from it in faith. Representations to the king and his ministers have hitherto remained unnoticed.

After his long imprisonment at Militsch, Pastor Krause was eventually banished to Erfurt, 80 miles from his own home, and there sentenced to an additional fine of 320 francs, or ten weeks' imprisonment, for having administered the sacrament in his official capacity.

The Lutheran community remaining faithful to the Confession of their forefathers, the State church now rages against them with greater violence. It has appointed policemen (gendarmen) on horseback, and permitted them on all occasions to use arbitrary power. With the assistance of a hired mob, the people have been violently dragged from the house of God, and besides this, have been fined in one instance 1328 francs (£53) for their mode of worship.

The communities have made a representation to the government, and proved their legal right; but instead of an answer, the police and commissioners were sent to distrain them as severely as they pleased, and were permitted to take away even the household provisions. Thus the police, the commissioners of taxes, the magistrates of the place, and a crowd of constables, acted like common robbers for a whole week in the village of Lutzeine, attempting even to take away the clothing from the bodies of the very poorest. Instead of the imposed £53, they robbed them of property amounting to £150, (3990 francs.) They carried away their robberies upon large carts. From a poor man in Uieschutz, they took away his whole provision for cattle, and also his cow, amounting together to 180 francs, (£7 5s.) Some other poor people they fined 160 francs, (£6 10s.) merely on account of having attended their places of worship. Many of those distrained have been reduced to beggary by these robbers. During the sale of their property, the poor people have been cruelly mocked by the commissioners and the police, but they have borne it all with patience, and opposed themselves not even with a word. This it is which mortifies the persecutors most, that the Lutherans, under all their oppressions, prove themselves so meek; and pay their taxes punctually and willingly, for their enemies would fain have a pretext for treating them as rebels. At last they cried out, "You are mad!"—"deprived of your senses!"—"you will be brought into madhouses," &c.

These are the deeds of the New State church, in the kingdom of Prussia, the land from which all other countries carry away wisdom and civilization, and that boasts of its spirit of toleration! Yes! blasphemy, atheism, and frivolity, are tolerated in the universities, in the pulpits, churches, and schools; but that church which has founded the existence of Prussia, and still maintains it, is not tolerated, but persecuted. The United Prussian State church has exacted above £360 (9000 francs) from the above mentioned community of the circles of Militsch, Trebnitz, and Wartenberg alone. Ten or twelve times that sum has been extorted from the other communities in Silesia; and if all the fines which have been exacted from the poor Lutherans since the year 1830 were put together, the sum may be computed to amount to at least £10,000, (250,000 francs.)

Every impartial man may justly ask the question, "Have not these persecuted Lutherans some dangerous political end in view?" No! for upon the inquiry of ministers, and other State officers, the answer from the best accredited local authorities has uniformly been, "They are the most quiet subjects, and perform their duties of allegiance most punctually and willingly; never yet has a Lutheran been punished on account of the non-performance of his secular duties." "Are the Lutherans demagogues?" No! for the Lutherans have boldly declared to the government, that among the hundreds of persons imprisoned for disaffection, there was not *one* Lutheran.

They challenged the ministry to point out to them *one* Lutheran that was a demagogue. Three years have passed, and the ministry have not yet given an answer to this.

"Or are the Lutherans criminals, murderers, thieves, impostors, calumniators, smugglers?" By no means!—for in no prison of the Prussian state is one single Lutheran to be found who has been punished for such a crime. "Are they then a new sect?" Most assuredly not; but the church which has existed for these three hundred years; it is the State church, on the contrary, which is a new sect. What then have the Lutherans done? Answer— No more than that they remain faithful to the church of their fathers, and for conscience' sake in matters of faith, adopt no state uniform—no state commandership—no visible head of the church— no pope—but simply adhere to the word of God. The Lutherans have petitioned for leave to emigrate, but the ministry refuse it, and say in reply, "That it is impudent to maintain that there is no liberty of faith and conscience in Prussia; that the government refuses to grant consent for emigration, and will know how to meet such obstinacy."

What must we feel at these assertions?—shall we weep, or give vent to our indignation, that authorities can unblushingly make assurances that are belied by their own fearful persecutions; assurances, the falsehood of which every one knows, and their evil deeds clearly prove? The peace of Westphalia guarantees to every subject in the whole of Germany and Prussia free emigration, if he cannot enjoy the unfettered exercise of his faith in his own country. On that basis (the peace of Westphalia) one hundred years ago, Prussia compelled the Archbishop of Saltzburg to grant consent for emigration previously refused to the persecuted Lutherans there, and Prussia received twenty thousand of them; and now, after a century has elapsed, Prussia herself adopts the same cruel policy.

The Lutherans are not allowed to emigrate, because the government is ashamed to have the disgrace of intolerance made known to the world. But the Almighty will be judge, and bring to light cruelties which in the nineteenth century appear incredible and unheard of. He will bring assistance to his sighing people. The peace of Westphalia is broken by the Prussian state; the laws of men, and the law of nations are broken, and yet it is maintained that Prussia rules with moderation and mildness. England has offered to assist the distressed Lutherans, and to grant them a free passage and support to Australia, but the Prussian state will not allow the Lutherans to leave, but punished them.*

* In the year 1836, the suffering Lutherans in Silesia were led to believe that the Prussian government would grant them passports for emigration; and one of their ministers, named Augustus Kavel, was sent as a deputation to England, to make arrangements on the subject with the South Australian Company. Those arrangements were completed; a large vessel was chartered by the company,

The above is but a slight sketch of the persecutions which the State church (not guaranteed by any previous rights) pursues towards the Lutheran to take them out, and Kavel's flock, to the amount of some hundreds, had already embarked on the Oder, for the purpose of joining this vessel at Hamburg, having previously settled their affairs, and disposed of their surplus goods; when a government order was received, commanding them to return to their homes, where they were kept in suspense for nearly two years, consuming that little property which should have served them for capital in a new country. In the mean time, the South Australian Company had obtained other labourers; and it was not to be expected that they should again incur the heavy responsibility of providing the means of emigration for these persecuted people. The Prussian government having at length granted the desired permission, in the year 1836, six hundred individuals were sent out to the colony, through the princely aid of a British merchant, who also, with true Christian hospitality, maintained the distressed pastor during the two years he was kept waiting in this country.

The following extract from a letter, addressed by Pastor Kavel to this gentleman, will show the delicate care with which the Lutherans have avoided any attempt to excite foreign interference. It is dated London, Oct. 25, 1837. "I think it my duty to inform you of my having been invited by Mr. ——, to attend the meeting, which was held on Thursday the 24th inst. by the London Ministers, in order to take into consideration the persecution in Prussia and Holland. Mr. —— kindly offered to introduce me, and desired me to lay my case before the Rev. Gentlemen. But I thought it my duty to decline this invitation, and thus I did not attend the meeting. Mr. —— was of opinion, that the meeting would resolve upon requesting the English government to ask the Prussian and Dutch government for a reason of these persecutions, and to request them to put a stop to such vexations. Not knowing whether the Rev. Gentlemen have taken such a church, guaranteed by rights of three hundred years' standing. "But judgment shall return unto righteousness, and all the upright in heart shall

resolution or not, I only beg leave to confess, that though, on the one hand, acknowledging the lively interest the London Ministers are taking concerning the persecution of their brethren, I consider it to be none of my business to lay the affairs of my congregation and brethren before the English public, and to wish in any way for political interference. And I believe all my brethren in Prussia are of the same opinion, trusting that the Lord will deliver us in His season, not by might nor by power, but by his Spirit. We, the Lutherans, think it not to be contrary to the word of God, to leave a country where our religious freedom is endangered; but we consider it inconsistent with the Scriptures to claim the interference of foreign power, because there is not the least hint given in the New Testament for acting thus. You know, my dear Sir, I came over to England to find a place of refuge for my flock; and now having found it by means of your assistance, I consider my business as settled, and am still hoping that the Prussian government will grant passports, observing our avoiding to procure us foreign political interference. In conclusion allow me simply to state, in a few words, the political sentiments of the Lutheran church, explained in the 28th article of the Augsburg Confession.

1st. We believe and confess that God Almighty has instituted two powers on earth—a political and an ecclesiastical one, or the state and the church, and that both of them are to be obeyed.

2nd. We believe that kings, authorities, magistrates, masters, and parents, rule by the grace of God, and that subjects, inferiors, and children, have to yield obedience for God's and conscience' sake, without asking for many reasons, yea, that they have to obey even the froward masters.—1 Peter ii. 18.

3rd. We believe and confess, that subjects, inferiors, and children, may claim their rights in a legal way, according to follow it."—Psalm xciv. 15. " For the Lord knoweth the way of the righteous."—Psalm i. 6. " For the arms of the wicked shall be broken; but the Lord upholdeth the righteous."—Psalm xxxvii. 7. " For the rod of the wicked shall not rest upon the lot of the righteous; lest the righteous put forth their hands unto iniquity."—Psalm cxxv. 3.

the law of the country; but if their claims be not attended to they are by no means allowed to help themselves, or to compel their superiors in any way to yield to their wishes.

4th. We believe that the political government is not allowed or privileged to interfere with ecclesiastical affairs, or to alter and injure the rights of the church, but bound as a Christian government to watch over the privileges of the church. And, on the other hand, that the church has no right to interfere nor mingle with the rights and privileges of the state, but to preach the gospel to all men, even to kings and authorities; but only to preach, not to exact obedience, because the kingdom of God is not of this world.

5th. We believe that if the state infringes on the privileges of the church, the church may try to defend her prerogatives by preaching, or in any lawful way, according to the laws of the country; but if government go on persecuting the church, she has not to claim foreign interference, or to take up arms for her defence, but may go on preaching and administering the Sacraments, and suffer till God is pleased to relieve her. And if the church choose, or be able to take refuge in a foreign country, as the Moravian brethren did one hundred and twenty years ago, we do not think this inconsistent with the Bible.

" Having cherished and entertained these sentiments of the Lutheran church hitherto, I never wish to give them up, and therefore I have nothing to do with any meeting that claims political interference." ED.

II.

In the beginning of the year 1837, a new Cabinet order appeared, which led the more just and humane portion of the Prussian subjects, to believe that the honour of their country might yet be retrieved by the abandonment of these arbitrary and cruel proceedings, which they were ready to conclude, could only have arisen from the machinations of hierarchical intrigue. This ordinance was to the following effect.

1st. No new prosecution sshall be commenced against the Lutherans, without the consent of the ministry of spiritual affairs.

2nd. The prosecutions now pending shall be closed, and judgments given, but the execution of judgment shall be suspended till the king shall have confirmed the same.

3rd. The Upper Court of Justice of Breslau, shall no longer give judgment in the present prosecutions, but the judgment already given shall not be reversed.

It was now expected that the true sentiments of the King would become known, and this was a cause of rejoicing to the military, and especially to the commissioned officers. Even among the soldiers, a Christian sympathy for the sufferers has been manifested, and though an attempt was made to bring their consciences also under sway, several commissioned officers have felt themselves constrained to return from the United Church, to the persecuted church of their forefathers. Among others, a captain of the 27th regiment of infantry, named Von Rohr. The same had had his child baptized by a Lutheran pastor, and given the legal notice for its registration. Inquisitorial examinations followed, against which, according to authentic information, Von Rohr addressed two petitions to the King. In the first, that he might not be required to name the pastor who baptized his child, knowing that this would subject him to fine and imprisonment; in the second, to be released from the duty of military church service, and the observance of the Lord's-supper in the united church, as he could not be present with an easy conscience. As an answer, he received a cabinet order, simply containing his discharge, on the ground of non-compliance with the legal prescriptions. The esteem and sympathy which his superiors and brethren in faith felt for this honourable man, who is without any earthly fortune, were truly touching.

Two Lutheran pastors from Silesia, whom they could no longer detain illegally in their prisons, were transported from thence to Erfurt.* An excellent and influential pastor residing there, named Grabau, when informed of these deeds, spoke openly from the pulpit against the persecutions, and said that he must return to the Lutheran church. Grabau was then suspended; but when a stranger rose in the pulpit, to praise publicly the new *Prussian charity, meekness, and moderation, while Prussian swords and bayonets were stationed in the church*, a general indignation showed itself, and it was only

---

* One of these was probably Pastor Krause. ED.

the decisive word of the suspended pastor, which succeeded to disperse the enraged multitude in peace.

The community in Thuringia and at Erfurt, petitioned the King to reinstate their pastor, or at least, to give them another Lutheran minister, as otherwise they must incorporate themselves with Pastor Grabau's congregation. The following facts served for an answer:

On the first of March, 1837, at three o'clock in the afternoon, Grabau was summoned before the magistrates, as it was pretended to give explanations. When he appeared, the Burgomaster declared to him that the government of Erfurt had determined to remove him from the town, as he did not submit to their commands respecting his pastoral functions. He was told that his removal must take place that very day. Grabau replied, that in that case he must first go home and procure the necessaries for his journey and future absence. The Burgomaster, who had previously affected much courtesy, and affirmed that *he* would never persecute people, then threw off the mask, for he locked the door, that Grabau might not go out, observing, "You may inform your wife of your wants in writing." The latter in consequence sent for his wife and only little son, twelve months old, informed her of the reasons for this, and named the things he wanted.

The good woman was much distressed, and hurried to the magistrates, accompanied by her servant. The Burgomaster played the man of the world towards the lady of the pastor, and affected sympathy by politeness and courteous manners; and upon the question, "whither was hér husband to be carried?" and "how would he be treated?" he replied, "Your husband will not be taken far from Erfurt, every thing is ready for his reception; he will find a healthy and comfortable room, and shall stand in need of nothing; in a few days you shall be informed of the place of his new residence." The lady pastoress having in her consternation forgot some of the things ordered by her husband, which he was much in want of, and the journey having to take place on a cold winter night, wished to have them fetched by her servant; but neither servant nor pastoress were allowed to leave, from a fear that the community might hear of their pastor being banished. The lady was appeased with the words, "it was not necessary to trouble herself, care would be taken of her husband, so that he would have no need of the things requested." The lady trusted the Burgomaster, for who would not trust to such a high and sworn officer, who had to remind others of faith and honesty. But this, as will be shown hereafter, was an intentional deception. When the time for departure drew near, Grabau prayed with his wife, and recommended her, his child, and the community, to the protection of God, the Father, Son, and Holy Ghost. During prayer, the Burgomaster and police retired hastily into another room.

When it became dark, the extra mail by which Grabau was to be sent away, was driven into the court-yard of the mayoralty house. The pastor was then delivered to a sergeant, a commissary of the police, named Rochlitz, who loudly boasted of being a free-thinker. The latter first placed his dagger in the carriage, then the pastor was obliged to get in, and the commissary of the police took his seat beside him. In order that no human eye might see the deed, the leather curtains of the carriage were buckled fast, though Grabau objected to this with the remark, "wherefore was it done? he was no criminal."

The people of Erfurt, who have spoken of this event, say that they remembered at the time the words of Holy Writ—" He that doeth evil hateth the light, neither cometh to the light, lest his deeds should be reproved."

The Burgomaster (mayor) had assured the wife of Grabau, that every attention should be paid to his comfort, and that he would not miss the things required. But this was not true. He was but partially covered with a light woollen blanket, and exposed to a draught and the severe cold of a winter night. Pastor Grabau's usual health is but delicate, and he was only provided with a light cloth coat, single boots, common hat, and light cloak. The sergeant sat carelessly by his side. When Grabau prayed on the road, the free-thinker felt great anguish, as he afterwards confessed.

Grabau soon became dangerously ill; being seized with cramp in the stomach and violent sickness, so that the sergeant had serious apprehensions that his victim might die before he could be brought into the prison. In order to prevent this, he offered him some warm beer; but it was refused from such an evil doer. On the second of March, a stay was made at Heiligenstadt. Here they intended to lock the pastor in a prison for criminals, the cell having scarcely half a window, barred up with iron rails; but he protested against this, and was afterwards brought into another apartment of larger size, but damp, and containing a bed, too dirty and disgusting to be used. Here he was obliged to do as well as he could. His food consisted of the same soup, both at dinner and supper, as was given to the criminals, and was consequently but ill suited to his weakly constitution.

These were therefore the comforts which the Burgomaster had promised to the wife of the pastor! It must also be remarked, in addition to the above, that he was not allowed to be alone, but a coarse felon was locked up with him, who chiefly spent his time in drinking and swearing. When the pastor endeavoured to impress him with the wickedness of such conduct, he one evening attempted to give him a severe beating. After some time, however, he left off swearing. Upon his return home, Rochlitz, the commissary of the police, spoke publicly, and with malicious joy, of the miserable place in which he had left Grabau. This news spread quickly through the whole town, and induced Grabau's wife to reproach the Burgomaster. The latter replied, "This is not the case, your husband is treated like a gentleman." In a letter to Erfurt, Grabau described his situation. As this letter had to pass through the criminal courts at Heiligenstadt, it was opened and read, and the contents were written upon the outside. The letter was then sealed, and sent to the government at Erfurt, which instead of removing the evil, sent the letter back to the prison of Grabau. Thus they wished to suppress the publication of their barbarous cruelty.

It is to be expected that a Christian minister finds hope and comfort within himself to strengthen him: but the community was also strengthened in its faith, and ready to remain firm, even to death. These events spread Lutheranism in the surrounding provinces. The imprisonment and treatment of Grabau became also known at Heiligenstadt, and Roman Catholics and members of the United Church, shewed unanimously their warmest sympathy.

This may form a small specimen of that toleration which has been practised in Prussia for several years past. German and foreign Christians and philanthropists, must not be astonished if many voices have not been raised in Germany against such cruelties; for it is well known, that the reading of Lutheran writings, much more the purchase of those which contain the present history, is punished in Prussia by a fine of 100 six-dollars. In some provinces, a reward of 50 rix-dollars is given to any post-master who discovers such a pamphlet passing through his hands. The restrictions, with respect to printing and the censorship of the press, are in accordance with these measures. As far back as the year 1827, it became known through the medium of princes themselves, that orders had been sent to all the German courts, partly in a polite, partly in a threatening, manner, not to allow any thing to appear in their respective lands against the Prussian state church.

The natural consequence of all this, has been the absence of correct and public information on the subject. A faithful account has appeared in a Danish town, under the title of "The newest history of the Lutheran church," by Dr. J. G. Scheibel, published at Altona. We recommend this excellent periodical to all our readers who may wish to hear more detailed particulars.

III.

THE pastors Kellner, Berger, Gessner and Biehler, are still in prison, (Kellner since 4th of October 1834.) Guerike, in Halle, is under town arrest. ——Zahn, Esq. at Turnowa, has been distrained for 200 rix dollars. In Gollnow, near Stettin, on account of a small fine they took the cows from the stable of the Lutherans there. The Countess Henkel of Donnersmark, and two noble ladies of Lobeck, both the daughters of a Prussian Major, have been condemned as rebels to a fort for one year! Many peasant women have also languished in prison on account of their Lutheran faith.

The persecution is becoming increasingly severe. The king has forbidden all public transactions with the Lutherans, and withdrawn their cause from the courts of justice, so that it is now entirely handed over to the police department. But these measures fail in their intended aim—the destruction of the Lutheran church. The persecutions have hitherto only rendered the Lutherans more firm and faithful, and a great number of those who had conformed, have left the State church, and again united themselves to those who remained true to their former faith. Thus new communities have arisen, not only in the circles of Silesia, but also in Pomerania, Posen, Magdeburg, Halle, and Berlin. The fine Christian character of the Lutheran, also contributes much to the increase of his church, for other fruits are produced by her than by the State church. The Lutherans have been purified by the fire of persecution, and are patterns of Christian excellence; being enabled to treat their persecutors with patience and meekness, for they are conscious of their own sinfulness, and this is a heavier burden to them, than all outward enemies and oppressions.

IV.

EVENTS which have taken place since the appearing of the Cabinet order of the 2nd of January, seem to prove that the destruction of the Lutherans is now to be effected by still more arbitrary measures. The following facts will show how this has been attempted.

About fifty poor country people in Silesia assembled for worship, and on account of this single religious assembly they were fined 330 dollars

(£50); their reader, moreover, was ill-treated by the police, and no attention was given to their appeal. These people had suffered severely from previous fines, but were now again distrained, and lost their all. The increase of the communities in the mean time, clearly proves that Satan, with all his power and cunning, cannot destroy the church of Christ, and that is our consolation. The church will not perish, though the most refined cruelties and attempts at seduction may be tried, for the Spirit of the Most High is within her, and she trusts to the promise of the Lord, that even the gates of hell shall not be permitted to prevail against her.

V.

THE following accounts have reached us, since the previous pages went to the press.

A circular signed by the ministry of spiritual affairs, and by that for the direction of the police, has been sent to the clergy of the State church, ordering them to give timely information to the magisterial authorities, and to seek by all other means in their power to prevent the spread of Lutheranism. These are the means used to convert the Lutherans from errors (if they be so), which have now existed for three hundred years. What wonder if many take to flight secretly! Ten families have already done so at Camin on the Baltic, because consent for emigration has been denied to them by government.

The following measures are particularly oppressive. Every child fourteen years of age, confirmed by a Lutheran pastor, is to be considered not confirmed, and therefore still subject to school visiting, so that the parents have to pay fines, which increase in geometrical progression, and for which they are distrained. A marriage, though published before the community when assembled at worship, on three consecutive Sundays, and announced in the newspapers, if solemnized by a Lutheran pastor, is to be considered null and void.

The appeals to the local royal governments are never attended to. The government of Bromberg has published in the official gazette of the 10th of February, (therefore long after the Cabinet order of the 2nd of January,) two decrees, according to which, every reader, and every one who lends his room for worship, shall be fined from three to five dollars, and every hearer, from one to three dollars, and in default of payment with proportionate imprisonment.

The children of Lutherans are to attend the religious instructions of the United Minister; in case of need their attendance is to be enforced by the police. They are to be re-confirmed, if only confirmed by a Lutheran pastor. In this case, guardians must be appointed for them, the same as for orphans. Fathers who refuse to have their children baptized in the State church, shall indemnify the minister of the place, besides paying a fine of from two to four dollars to the Exchequer.

Every Lutheran pastor who administers baptism shall pay a fine of fifty dollars. But the worst is that re-baptism is commanded.

VI.

Our beloved Gerkendorf, a non-commissioned officer, was imprisoned on Palm Sunday, 1837, because he declared, that he could no longer conscientiously attend the garrison church parades. He receives bread and water three times a day, and on the fourth day, something warm. No one is allowed to visit him. When he was brought for the first time before the court, his captain, who had exerted himself, earnestly on his behalf, for he was an excellent soldier said to him, "Dear Gerkendorf! what grief and disgrace you are bringing on the company! Just say to the examiner, that you had lost your senses, and you will be immediately released without punishment!" Gerkendorf replied; "Captain! the Almighty has given me understanding in this divine and glorious cause, to know the truth in the Lutheran church, and therefore will I confess it, even under tribulation—his will be done!" Gerkendorf said, that when he was cross-examined, his faith became somewhat weaker, but when he quoted the word of God, and the symbolical writings before the court, the gentlemen present began to cry out—"Why do you refer to the word of God?—Why do you speak of the symbolical writings?—Why do you keep talking of the Bible?" Gerkendorf remarked, that, at these words a beam of the glory of God shone upon his heart, so that he joyfully told them, "If the word of God will no longer avail a Christian before this court, then take away my life,—behead me at once."*

VII.

The Lutheran community in Berlin, is strong in the Lord, and receives new members daily. Pastor Lasius resides there since last January.* In the month of March, 1837, Kleinert and Hoffman, were commissioned by the Lutherans to present a petition to the Minister of the Police, supplicating for the entire liberty of Pastor Lasius; but they were sharply treated by the minister. He asked them, "What have you to complain of? Are you persecuted?" Hoffman replied, "Is there no persecution sir, in our Pastor Ehrenstrom being torn from us, and imprisoned? Pastor Lasius is sought for in our houses, as if he were a criminal; and thus all the Lutheran Pastors are unlawfully persecuted by the State, though they, like the rest of the Lutherans, are good and most faithful subjects." The minister became enraged at this reply of Hoffman's. With furious looks, he told both

---

* The following are the "Symbolical Books," and Confessional Writings," to which reference is so frequently made. The "Confession of Augsburg;" the "Apology for the same;" the "Articles of Smalkald; the "Little," and "Larger Catechism," of Dr. Martin Luther; and the "Concordia," published in the year 1580.

* Recent accounts of Pastor Lasius, have mentioned his now being in prison, and in want.—Ed.

Hoffman and Kleinert to be silent. But they were not afraid, for confidence in their God made them strong. The minister said, " I stand here in the name of the King, and you must obey his command. It is not for you to form a judgment about the legality or illegality of your pastor's imprisonment. It is enough, that you are rebels against the will of His Majesty, and for this you shall be punished." Both the dear brethren referred to the word of God, and the symbolical writings, saying, " We cannot act otherwise." At length he became satisfied.

On the 11th of March, Hoffman was again brought before the police. The examination lasted for two hours. The Lord Jesus endued him with his grace, so that he looked more cheerful than the Counsellor of the police. The latter was vexed that Hoffman looked so tranquil and cheerful. Dunker the Counsellor said to him, " You are a citizen of the State, a good Christian, and a servant of the King; all this will induce you to tell me the truth." " Yes," replied Hoffman, " as far as the word of God, and my conscience will allow me to do so." The following conversation then took place.

Counsellor. " Who is Pastor Kaul, that has baptized eight children in this town, and where does he live? This you must tell me."

Hoffman. " Sir! You were pleased just now to say, that I was a good Christian, for which you give us Lutherans credit, because we are faithful, both to our God, and to our King. But should I be a good Christian if I were to betray our Pastors, who are in bonds and imprisonment? If I were to inform against the brethren, should I not commit a Judas-like sin?"

Counsellor. "A sin like Judas?—I do not see that. Did not Christ voluntarily meet his enemies? He did not hide himself from the Authorities, as your pastors do."

Hoffman. "Yes! Christ the Lord went to meet his enemies, when the time of his suffering for our sins drew near; and thus, neither will his children and servants withdraw themselves from persecution for his name's sake, when the hour of suffering shall approach. But for the present, we live in a Christian country where there are still laws, by virtue of which the Lutheran church has existed for these three hundred years, and been the means of affording to the Prussian State, both, temporal and spiritual blessings.

When Hoffman reminded the Counsellor of the 16th Article of the Confession of Augsburg, not knowing what to reply, he began to speak of something else, saying, "The apostles did not hide themselves as your preachers do, but confessed freely before the magistrates." Hoffman replied, "excuse me, sir,—when Paul preached Christ at Damascus, where he was persecuted, he was let down by his brethren through a window from the city wall, which we consider to be in accordance with the advice of Jesus to his followers to seek for the wisdom of the serpent. The proceedings with pastor Ehrenstorm have taught us, how, in order to be guided by the word of God, we must now act with reference to the concealment of our pastors." Here the Counsellor began to speak of Luther saying, "Luther had not been so obstinate as we and our preachers; *he* had not crept into a corner, but went cheerfully to Worms. Hoffman replied, "With respect to Luther and his doctrine he says himself, 'As to what refers to faith and the word of God, I will show a bold front as hard as an anvil or diamond. I will not yield, though all the empires of the world should go to ruin by my steadfastness.' When the interdiction was afterwards laid upon Luther, and his life became endangered, did not the Elector prince keep him prisoner a whole year at the Castle of Wartburgh? If our pastors had the support of temporal princes as Luther had, they certainly would not hide themselves." The Counsellor of the Police then wished to know where the Lutherans concealed their church-books, and where the eight fathers of families lived, who had lately had their children baptized. When he failed in gaining an answer to these questions, he remarked,—"How can the State exist longer with such obstinate people!" Hoffman, "Sir! the state has existed for these three hundred years, and the Lutheran doctrine has not only not injured it, but has benefited it much—very much indeed." Counsellor, "You have written a letter to the former Pastor, Lasius, at Gumbinnen, and pressingly requested him to come here; in consequence of this letter he has come to this town; where is he now?" Hoffman, "Lasius has not come, in consequence of my letter. When my letter arrived at Gumbinnen, he had already left the place, otherwise the letter addressed to him would not have fallen into your hands." When this examination was finished, they conversed together for about an hour and a half, the Counsellor remarking, "This I tell you, if you do not change your sentiments, you can no longer remain a royal servant, but must be discharged." Hoffman, "If a Christian state can act thus towards one who has served it faithfully and honestly for twenty-four years, and is provided with the best testimonials for the whole time of his doing so; then the Almighty in whom I believe, will take care of me." In conclusion, the Counsellor remarked, "After all, faith is a very uncertain thing, one can never know which is the right faith!" Hoffman, "Sir, we Christians should be deceived indeed, if we had not a most sure and heavenly confidence, as to which is the true faith.—If we were to die this very moment, whither would our spirits go?" Here he became quite silent, and seemed deeply moved; then he said, "I believe that you are in the right, and yet you are much to be pitied; for instance, the eight children that have lately been baptized, can never receive any office in the state, when they are grown up, for their names are not inscribed in the Church register authorised by the state." Hoffman, "We care first for their spiritual well-being; but we hope that long before the children shall be old enough for civil service, the Lutheran Church will have re-obtained toleration in the Prussian State, and be authorised by the same.

Hoffman then placed before him the injustice of deposing Dr. Scheibel, Kellner, and other Pastors, adding this final remark: "We are not seduced by our Pastors, as you suppose; but you see that we possess a living faith in the word of God and in our confessional writings, which so beautifully harmonize with the Bible. Hoffman then addressed the brethren, reminding them how good it is to believe with all the heart, in the Lord Jesus, the Lord of glory, and also in the Holy Trinity, subsequently remarking, "Disagreeable and vexatious as this examination was to my flesh and blood, so glorious the word and doctrine of our Lord Jesus, and the confession of our church afterwards appeared to me, I would cheerfully lay down my life, if the Lord were to require it. Honour and glory be to him and his holy name, from me a poor sinner!"

We must here conclude, in order that this little work may not become too large for extensive circulation, among those whose means are limited. We would, finally beseech our brethren to follow the example of the Prussian Lutherans, whose faith, confession, character, and mode of life are truly scriptural, and a living representation of primitive Christianity. We especially entreat the brethren to love the Lord with all fervency, and from love to him, to believe in and obey his words, avoiding sectarianism, and remaining faithful to the ancient Christian church, which Luther re-established in its purity. We entreat them also, to afford pecuniary assistance to the oppressed brethren, as well as to pray often and fervently on their behalf. The smallest gift will be most gratefully received. Besides the editor, the following kind friends, will receive contributions for the persecuted Lutherans.*

Concluding Remarks.

The preceding accounts have been gathered from several clergymen, and laymen, from various countries. Every one gave me his information without knowing that I should receive additional particulars from other quarters. Some correspondents do not even know, that I have copies of their reports in my hands, and yet all their histories agree with each other. Several facts were related verbally by a friend, who visited me; a member of the Prussian Lutheran church. He confirmed all the written news I had received, particularly respecting the inhuman treatment which Pastor Grabau suffered; at the same time he told me that he is now treated more mildly. It is true he is still in prison at Heiligenstadt, and without the least prospect of speedy release; but he is now in possession of a more healthy room and better bed, and may go out daily, accompanied by a policeman; which the imprisoned Pastors in Silesia are not allowed to do. The last information I received of him was from the Superintendent of Saxony, a few days since.

* Here follow the names of several individuals, residing at Strasburg, Baden, and other places.

He remarked, "The beloved Pastor Grabau writes with great cheerfulness from his prison at Heiligenstadt; he says, he knows that it is the Lord alone, who has the keys of hell and death; he is still enabled to remain firm, and his community do so likewise; no threatening or allurement has hitherto been able to withdraw them from their faith."

I have left to every one who has given me information, his own mode of expression, in order that readers may see, by the difference of style, that the preceding accounts were received from various individuals. They will also observe, that several additional facts are inserted in the later sections, which I did not possess at the commencement of the statement. Allowance will be made for occcasional negligence of style, when it is seen, that the accounts were not drawn up for publication. Finally, I have only to remark, that the friends whose reports I have here communicated, are upright, pious, and conscientious people, on whose testimony the most entire reliance may be placed. All the narrated facts are true, though they are not allowed to be published in Prussia. Prussian official authorities, and newspaper editors, are shameless enough to deny them; as has lately been done by a Berlin editor, in a letter to Strasburg. Some Prussian intriguers have sought to prevent the publication of the present work, and have even offered an indemnification to induce me to suppress it. Many are too cowardly to witness to the truth, because they are afraid of losing their office and salary. An impartial judgment can as little be expected, from an official Prussian authority, as from an American planter, with respect to the treatment of his slaves. These authorities also, keep up connection with others in foreign countries, who are constantly on the watch, to prevent the publication of such writings, or, if they do appear, they represent them as calumnious, by the newspapers or other means. They audaciously and unblushingly deny the plainest facts. It will not therefore be surprising, if this pamphlet should share the same fate. If a man blindly and fanatically devoted to the Prussian Government, or a cowardly flatterer, should choose to deny the facts related in this little work; or to describe the Lutherans, as fanatics, sectarians, or rebels; he would undoubtedly receive a great reward.

M. ERNST.

Translated from the German, by J. D. L.

CHAPTER VIII.

KING OF PRUSSIA'S REFUSAL TO RECEIVE THE DEPUTATION FROM SILESIA.

Address of the Deputies to Pastor Diemer of Strasburg.

"LET us not be weary in well doing; for in due season we shall reap if we faint not. As we have therefore opportunity, let us do good unto all men, especially unto those who are of the household of faith."—GALATIANS vi. 9, 10.

Hamburgh, 20th April, 1839.

Beloved and revered friend and brother in our Lord Jesus Christ!

Your kind sympathy with our sufferings and persecutions has come to our knowledge by your writings, in which you make such a touching appeal for the charitable support of the persecuted Lutheran brethren in Prussia. In consequence of this, we take the liberty of sending you this address; and as our earlier persecutions are pretty well known to you, we have only to observe that the same have increased in many respects.

It is true that formerly we always cherished a hope, that if our severe persecution were brought by deputation to the ears of the King, it would come home to his heart, and he would be induced to protect and assist us. But, at the end of August, 1837, when such a deputation (of which the author of this address was a member) arrived at

Berlin, and on Monday the 28th of August, had presented a short petition for a personal audience, or, if this were not admissible, for permission to present our trials of faith and conscience, in a longer address in writing, no result followed for a whole week.

During this time, a representation of our sufferings, with an account of the persecution, and a supplication for redress, were prepared to be presented to his Majesty; and the Counsellor of the Cabinet, Müller, and the royal chaplain, Dr. Strauss, as Presiding Counsellor in the Consistory, were personally requested to lay our humble petition before the King. Dr. Strauss was told by one of the deputies, in taking farewell of him, while pressing his hand fervently, that it surely became him to act uprightly as court preacher.

On Sunday the 3rd of September, Pastor Lasius preached a sermon, and administered the Lord's-supper in the dwelling of the bailiff of the Lutheran congregation. The police traced us, and after the service was over, took the minister with the deputies to the police office, where we were individually examined in the roughest manner, and asked who had induced us to form such a deputation. In reply, it was alleged that the cruel persecutions, fines, imprisonments, the seizure of our cattle, household furniture, and implements of husbandry, solely on account of our constant adherence to the Lutheran creed and mode of worship, which have been authorised by law for the last three hundred years, were sufficient inducements to the step we had taken. At the conclusion of this examination, a law was read to every one individually, forbidding any deputation to the King. We were commanded to desist from it, according to this law, and told to return home immediately. Upon this, some members of the deputation steadfastly declared that they could not yield until they had executed their charge, according to the mandates of the Lutheran communities that had sent them, and had obtained an answer from his Majesty; our Lutheran church rites not only being founded on the Prussian state laws, but upon the treaties of peace, and other privileges obtained by the Diet of the empire. Then these individuals were carried off to prison, and on the following day again advised by the police magistrate to go quietly home. But when this was found to be fruitless, the conveyance tickets were written out, and we were told that the King had given orders to this effect. When we wished to see the royal command, the President of the Police replied that it was in higher hands, and assured us, upon his word of honour, "The ministry have resolved that you shall leave Berlin as soon as possible;" and that when this resolution was laid before the King, he had erased, with his own hand, the phrase, "as soon as possible," and substituted instead the word "forthwith."

Upon this, on the 5th of September, at five o'clock in the morning, we were put into a coach, accompanied by two policemen, in civil dress, on horseback; we were brought twelve miles, from Berlin to Frankfort on the Oder, where we received orders to return home according to the route given us.

In the mean time, the representation of our unjust persecution, and the supplication for redress made by the deputies, had reached the King, who handed it over without reply to the Ministerial Consistory. But the latter, in a judicial answer sent to us, called our complaints (which plainly rest on matters of fact,) criminal inventions and lies which we were daring enough to bring before the throne of his Majesty; and we were threatened for the future with the hardest usage, should it become necessary to proceed against us according to the power of the law.

This induced us, at the close of the year 1837, in an assembly where several wardens and members of the parishes of Trebnitz, Oelsne, Wartenberg, and Militsch, were present, to deliberate what, under such circumstances, was to be done; having first addressed fervent prayers to the Lord for his guidance and direction.

In consequence, it was unanimously resolved, to send again a representation to the Consistorial Ministry, in which single facts were repeatedly brought before them, as follows:—

In the first place, that the Lutheran church is disturbed by violence, the police dragging the hearers away by force, even during the reading of the sermon; and when the doors are closed, in order to prevent such evils, then the violence is increased. At Juliusburg, in the dwelling of Bierosch the weaver, the policeman, Winzig, used a wood-axe, with which he broke open the door of the room, like a thief and murderer. With the help of his assistants, he dragged out all the congregation, even while the sermon was being read, though he had been present at the commencement of the service, and taken down the names of all who attended; and had therefore absented himself for three quarters of an hour, merely in order to have more assistance for his sinful work. Upon this the worshippers of God (not the disturbers of the worship) were punished by the superior authorities with heavy fines. The penalties, on account of the Lutheran church service, in the village of Lutziene alone, amount to above three thousand dollars, and this is only the third part of those that are yet to be levied. The Lutherans in Great Tschunkawe have been subjected to such heavy fines, on account of adhering to their mode of worship, that many have lost the whole produce of their year's labour. Fathers of families, and widows, have been thrown into long imprisonment,—have been robbed of their property, clothing, house-utensils; of their cattle; nay, even of their ploughs. And these were distrained and sold by auction, solely because baptism and confirmation were performed by Lutheran pastors. The child of Cattert at Dunkawe, baptized by a Lutheran pastor, was brought by the policeman Berg, to the United Minister Butzki, at Suhlaw, in order to be re-baptized. In the same manner, the above-mentioned policeman, Berg, by the authority of the Magistrates of the village of Schwiebedawe, took away the child of a blacksmith, named Kreisel, who lives there, which was only six months old; and though it had been previously baptized by a Lutheran pastor, it was brought to Militsch for re-baptism, which was accordingly administered by Richter, the royal superintendant residing there.

These were the unvarnished facts we laid before them; and, at the conclusion, we begged that an end might be put to these dreadful evils; that the free independency of our Lutheran church might be granted, and that our imprisoned teachers and fathers of families might be restored to their liberty, or that, otherwise, free permission to emigrate might be given us. The first two requests have been entirely rejected by a decree, dated 2d March, 1838; and with respect to the leave for emigration, we were told to address ourselves to the proper royal authorities.

A great number soon determined to do so, as it appeared very clear to us, that the State church is not ruled by the Holy Ghost according to the Scriptures, but, contrary to the Divine word, by the arm of flesh; and under the sanction of merely human laws, punishes all who oppose it with imprisonment and banishment. As this new church government is against the word of God, and contradicts it, we will rather fly from such violent antichristian dominancy than live longer under it in continued trouble of conscience. For though we ourselves, through Divine mercy, might be enabled to stand firm to our principles, yet our children are torn from us by the police, and with violence brought into their schools, in order to be educated there according to their own views. Some who have even passed their fourteenth year, and been confirmed by Lutheran pastors, are taken by the police to the United schools, or to the State minister for examination, in order that, by the semblance of right, they might be incorporated with their church, or be made subject to it; and this took place after our remonstrances against their heavy fines had been long and loudly reiterated. Every father of a family and every widow, who omitted to send such children to school as had been confirmed by a Lutheran pastor, were fined five dollars per month, or adequate imprisonment. Considering our children as the dearest and most noble pledges confided to us by God, with the commandment to educate them in the nurture and admonition of the Lord, we can no longer live with a quiet conscience under such violent dominancy. To this must be added our own hungering and thirsting after the living preaching of the Divine word, after public worship and the holy sacraments, which under such persecution are but sparingly distributed, as almost all our preachers are imprisoned. This distress is aggravated when we consider the present state of our Lutheran church. Roused from its lethargy by the attempted Union, it has begun a new life, and a new epoch, in which, like a tender babe, it will pine and perish without the maternal nourishment of faithful doctrines. But the Prussian State authorities, who constitute likewise the rulers of the church, have only one end in view, which is that of extinguishing this new-born life, by depriving it of spiritual nourishment. We therefore hold ourselves justified in following the advice of our Lord Jesus, (Matthew, x. 23.) "When they persecute you in this city, flee ye into another." For though these words chiefly concern the apostles and teachers, yet we have also the example of the early Christians, who were enjoined to separate themselves from whatever was inconsistent with the Divine precepts. See Acts viii. 1, also Revelations xviii. 4, &c. And though we should rejoice to continue in communion with those in our native land who faithfully uphold the spirituality of true religion, yet without a compromise of principle it seems impossible to do this, and we have therefore resolved to emigrate.

We must, however, openly acknowledge, that many of our brethren in faith do not agree with us in this view of the subject; some, having no inward conviction, fear to do that which may not be right in the sight of the Lord, whilst others, including many of the preachers and chief persons in Breslau stand in the way; not that they consider the Lutheran church to be free, but still cherish a hope that it may obtain toleration. *We do not wait for this.* The persecution presses most heavily and severely upon the poor of our flock; who, bowed down under such a yoke of both bodily and spiritual thraldoms, sigh continually for liberty and redemption, yet find no means of relief.

Our poverty also renders it difficult to get away; for though there are many who have sold their houses and fields, and given the money obtained from the sales for the service of the poor, yet this will not suffice, as there are still many who have nothing at all, not even the necessary clothing. On the other hand, there are many who are not yet prepared to leave their well-stored households; who, perhaps, do not realize with filial confidence, the promise of our Lord, Mark x. 29, 30, "There is no man that hath left house, or brethren, or sister, or father, or mother, or wife, or children, or lands, for my sake and the gospel's, but he shall receive an hundredfold," &c.

By the kind providence of God, a considerable number of our brethren have already been liberated, and been brought by unforeseen assistance to South Australia, whither our dear Pastor Krause intended to follow them.* We sent him to Hamburgh, with two other brethren to make arrangements for our own departure; but finding difficulties in the way of going to South Australia, he and one of his companions proceeded to North America, where they arrived on the 7th of January, after a very tempestuous voyage. From

* The particulars connected with these interesting emigrants and their settlement in South Australia, will probably appear, ere long, in another volume.

thence they inform us, that without pecuniary means it will be utterly impossible to settle there, as a community; the tracts of land which are easily cultivated being already in the hands of usurers, and the government allowing no loan of money, nor any other assistance. We therefore direct our attention to other colonies; but at present stand, like the Israelites on the shores of the Red Sea, when they did not yet know how God would enable them to cross it.

Having now commended our situation to your Christian sympathy and love, in a few words, we merely add the humble request, that if in consequence of your powerful appeal, some support should have come in, by which the hearts of our poor exiles would be rejoiced, you will be pleased to send the same immediately to Hamburgh; for above one hundred and fifty individuals are already upon their journey from Silesia to this town. They do not yet know how, or whither they are to go; and for many of them the most indispensable necessaries are still to be provided. We shall not be able to depart from hence before the middle of May; but should your kind contributions arrive too late to meet us, the next company that emigrate would be benefited by them. We beg to have them directed to Mr. Heyn, wine merchant, Hamburgh. We have known him for several years as a faithful witness for the truth; and he has made great sacrifices on behalf of our persecuted brethren, as they have passed through Hamburgh. We, as well as those who are to follow us, would gratefully rejoice to receive assistance from the inhabitants of Breslau, who seem to have shut their hearts to their brethren in faith, because they emigrate against their will. They still hope for public toleration from Prussia; but, considering the uncertainty of this, we find no justification in holy writ for exposing ourselves, in the mean time, to the temptations that surround us. Quite the reverse. Abraham was commanded to go into a foreign land; Lot to fly from Sodom, in order to save his soul; yea, our Saviour himself, as our chief pattern, was removed in his tender childhood beyond the power of him who aimed at his life.

We now conclude, recommending you to the grace of our God and Saviour, and with grateful thanks, and again requesting your Christian sympathy and prayers, remain your obliged brethren in the Lord,

CHRISTIAN GOTTLIEB BIEROSCH,
JOSEPH HANSCHKE,
CARL BENJAMIN SCHULTHES. *

* This congregation received some pecuniary assistance from Christian friends in London, during its stay at Hamburgh, and finally procceded to North America.—ED.

Translated from the German, by J. D. L.

CHAPTER IX.

FAREWELL ADDRESS OF THE EMIGRANTS TO SOUTH AUSTRALIA.

On board the Catharine, at Cuxhaven, Sept. 21st, 1838.

We, the undersigned, elders of the Congregation emigrating from Posen, with the salutation of peace, return our hearty thanks to all friends, acquaintances, and benefactors, at Hamburgh, Barmbeck, St. George, and other neighbouring places, for the undeserved love we have experienced during the whole time we have been a burden to you.

Now, on the point of sailing, we do so, in the name of young and old, fathers and mothers, children and sucklings. May God, the bountiful distributor of all good gifts, reward you richly, both in this world, and in the world to come. May he, the Lord Jesus, grant you a never-fading crown, and place you on his right hand, in that kingdom where joy and bliss last for ever and ever.

We now leave our father-land with this last farewell to our country. Once more, we look back, at this very serious hour, upon the circumstances under which we part. Why do we leave our native land? We seek not that liberty which this earthly perishable existence can afford. Convinced that the truth in Christ Jesus can alone make eternally free, our only reason for emigrating is this—that we may continue a truly evangelical community, founding our liberty, not upon the permission of man, but upon the authority of scriptural truth; and we adhere to that view of scriptural truth which Luther upheld, because we believe it to be the true one. We cannot therefore, adopt the uniform prayer-book (agenda) which has been drawn up for the use of the Reformed and Lutheran Churches. Moreover, by the removal of Lutheran pastors from their flocks, the latter become dissolved, like companies of soldiers who are put into other regiments. The most important part of the case is therefore this,—we could not submit to this system of incorporation; but remained faithful to our pastors, as our pastors to us, and both to the uncorrupted Lutheran church service; and we have therefore concluded, that though we are no separatists, as we are unjustly called, yet we cannot conscientiously unite with the newly formed church, but must simply adhere to our own long-established views of scriptural truth, to which we cling with an inward and ardent love. We do but therefore attach ourselves to Luther, as many of our departed but honoured sovereigns (gottseligen Landesherren) have done before us, particularly that noble confessor of his faith, Margrave George of

Brandenburgh, who said, "I am not baptized into Luther,—he is neither my God, nor my Saviour—I do not believe in him—I shall not be saved through him—in this sense I am not a Lutheran:—but if I am asked, whether I hold in my heart, and profess with my life, that doctrine which God again brought to light by the instrumentality of Dr. Luther, then I have no hesitation to acknowledge—no aversion to call myself a Lutheran—and in this sense I am, and shall ever remain, a Lutheran, and herein I separate myself from all sects, whether Papists, Sacramentalists, Anabaptists, or others.

It is not with angry feelings, not with contempt for others, that we have been induced to take this step, but simply from the conviction that it is neither safe nor advisable to do any thing against one's conscience, and from an ardent desire to follow our Saviour in all things, and on no account to bring secret reserves into the sanctuary, or double-meaning words before the altar; for it is there that the force of Christian truths is most powerfully felt; and woe unto him who does not there acknowledge their importance.

We desire those who wished us to act contrary to our consciences, but could not succeed in their efforts, to consider two things: First, the simple and wholly filial fidelity of the Lutheran church to the Divine word. Secondly, the manly resolution with which the speculations of men with respect to the Divine word are rejected; and that its doctrines, as to the general election of grace, the

Lord's-supper, and Baptism, are all drawn directly from the Bible.*

We earnestly desire that the honoured and excellent ministers who are now in prison, may be restored to their communities. They have cheerfully sacrificed tranquillity, advancement, revenue, nay, even personal liberty, for conscience sake, and their own inward peace. We pray that they may be allowed to resume the care of the souls confided to them, and be permitted to serve their God freely, publicly, and without molestation, as their forefathers have done before them.

Finally, we earnestly desire, not only that these steadfast men of God may be liberated, but that a free Lutheran Consistory may be allowed; because candidates for the ministry in connection with our Church, can only be properly examined by a Consistory of members of the Lutheran faith. This appears too clear to admit of a doubt upon the subject, but alas! we have learned to our cost, that a strict adherence to the dictates of conscience is unknown to many influential persons, and has been suppressed in others by worldly expediency and the fear of man.

These things were laid before Dr. Strauss, the Counsellor of the United Consistory, in our interview with him, on the 6th of July, 1838. Dr. Strauss sought to convince us, by Rom. xiii. 1, 2,

* In giving expression to sentiments on controverted points, the editor wishes not to be held responsible for their correctness, though admiring the conscientious steadfastness with which they are maintained.

5, 6. that we were disobedient subjects; but we could not see that, as we were provided with the best testimonials, by the Magistrates, and other authorities of the place to which we belonged, as to all things which concerned our obedience to government in secular matters; and as to religious ones, surely no earthly power has a right to bear sway over our consciences. This same gentleman laid much stress on some Latin words, which we remember, though we did not understand them. These words were "Jus in sacra," and "Jus circa sacra." To this we replied, that if Latin were to be the tongue, our pastors, (many of whom are still in prison) must first be called together, our Lutheran Pastor understanding Latin. It cannot be required that we should allow those to speak for us in the interpretation of Latin, who are not of our faith.

Our ministers have often, and with many tears, exhorted us on no account to deviate from the past decisions of the Lutheran Consistories, for that they believed that we could not do so without danger to our most precious faith. We have pledged our word that it shall be so, and must abide by the same. Our wishes appeared to us, the more just in consideration of our blameless conduct.

But the time for granting our request was not yet come, and we were therefore obliged to emigrate. Owing to his continued imprisonment, our own beloved pastor is at present unable to accompany us; but he will follow as soon as he can.

We now conclude: If the conforming consistories are sure of the righteousness of their cause they have nothing to fear from the liberation of the Lutheran Pastors, nor from the Consistory to which the latter are lawfully entitled. But should this just request not be granted, it will not only be against the peace of Westphalia, and all confirmed privileges of the Lutherans, but also against the most simple rules of Christian sympathy and love. This view of the subject is also consistent with scriptural truth, and with the articles of the Confession of Augsburg.

Oh! that Bible truth *alone* might be loved in our father-land, as the fountain of light and justice, and might be loved indeed, and not merely in word! Then the maxims of men, and an improper secular authority, will no longer be allowed to rule over the conscience; then the true nobility of the soul,—that liberty which Christ bestows, will not be lost sight of; but truth and conscientiousness, displayed in our walk before our fellow-creatures, will again bless the land; then charity and faith will meet each other, and justice and peace be united in brotherly embrace. Oh! that this may be fulfilled, and that we may hereafter be permitted to meet them we are leaving behind at the right hand of the Lord Jesus! Once more, we bless his name and say, Glory be to the Lord of Sabaoth in all the corners of the earth!

JOHANN GEORGE JASCHKE,
CHRISTIAN ROTHE,
CHRISTIAN KAPPLER.

Translated from the German by J. D. L.

CHAPTER X.

ADMIRABLE CONDUCT OF THE EMIGRANTS, WHILE AT HAMBURGH.

Extract of a letter from a gentleman residing in Hamburgh, Aug. 21, 1839.

It will be most acceptable to you to learn how remarkably well these poor people behave, and how great an interest has been excited in many quarters, in their favour. They are residing at Barmbeck, a village about two English miles from the gates; where a benevolent farmer, (I think he is an Englishman by birth) has given them a large out-house, gratis, during their stay here. With any other body of men, the public authorities would have opposed difficulties to their thus domiciliating themselves, as it were, in this small State; but the good feeling which exists in various quarters towards them, has induced these authorities, if not actually to assent to the innovation, at all events to wink at it. These worthy people do all they can to fulfil their part, during the delay which has necessarily occurred. Some of them have been continually employed in the fields by the neighbouring farmers. Others have occupation as masons, carpenters, &c. and there is decidedly a disposition on the part of all, to assist them to the extent of their limited means. During the time the Zebra was lying off Altona, the vessel was regularly visited every evening, by from thirty to forty inhabitants of the town, drawn out for the purpose of being witnesses of, and participating in, the religious observances of the emigrants; and the surrounding vessels were crowded at the same regular periods, by their own crews, as well as strangers, all eager to enjoy the quiet melody of their evening hymns. On such occasions, many little acts of kindness were shown to the emigrants, small presents of useful articles made, and the children regaled with plain cakes.

I understand it is just the same at Barmbeck, where the evening vespers of the emigrants are as attractive among the surrounding peasantry, as those of their friends of the Zebra were among the towns-people of Altona."

CHAPTER XI.

VOYAGE TO SOUTH AUSTRALIA.

BRETHREN! tarrying here and there,
Till the Morning Star arise—
   Christ himself arise!
Quickly, quick, your lamps prepare,
Trimm'd with oil in fresh supplies;
Lighted thus ere day shall spring,
Guests, go in unto your King.

Who the good kind King has known,
That for us was smitten so,
   In that hour of woe,
When life's Lord, by death o'erthrown,
Bound for us, was bow'd so low—
With the Altar's incense send
Heartfelt praise to such a Friend!

J. L. F.

Adelaide, South Australia, Jan. 27, 1839.

Beloved and much esteemed brethren and fellow-countrymen.

It would have afforded me pleasure to have addressed you earlier from this remote part of the world; but I have been prevented by various circumstances, the chief of which was, the expense of sending a letter by way of England.

I return in spirit once more to Prussia, my

former country, and will now depict to you, briefly and simply, as in one continued scene, the particulars of our voyage, which was in many respects a remarkable one.

You, who are from Karga and its neighbourhood, witnessed our departure at Tschicherzig, near Yullicau; from whence we commenced our voyage, imploring blessings on the many sympathizing individuals whom we noticed amongst our neighbours and countrymen; and conscious of the important step we were taking, we sailed smoothly along on the beautiful surface of the Oder. We felt particularly invigorated and happy, and loosened as it were from every tie. It seems to me, that, in some respects, this sublime feeling of freedom can only be experienced where there is a similar resolution to emigrate. It was very perceptibly felt by us; for when an individual who has striven to live blamelessly in the sight of the world and the government, especially when he has attained to an advanced age, is scarcely permitted to occupy a decent dwelling in his own country, because he professes to belong to the Lutheran church, and until lately could not even obtain a passport to enable him to leave the country, but at length receives it, with sundry sarcastic remarks from the magistrates, and is obliged to resolve upon a voyage of fifteen thousand miles—is not this a stupendous undertaking, and must not the Lord grant great and unwonted courage for such an enterprise? And the Lord did so in our case; for the more we had to endure in Prussia because of our Lutheranism, and the more repeated the attempts to stop our mouths from uttering the Lutheran confession, the more joyfully did our hymns and sermons and prayers ascend in the open air, above the watery expanse, to the Lord of heaven and earth *.

* A German song used by the Saltzburg pilgrims a century ago, may be not inappropriately inserted here, permission having been kindly given by the translator. It will be remembered that in many respects their circumstances resembled those of the modern Lutherans.

I AM a poor, poor exile here,
  Without a friend or home—
Driven from my mother-country dear,
  For sake of God to roam.

But well I know, ah! Jesus, Lord,
  This happened too, to thee!
Thy will be done—and now, O Lord!
  Thy follower I will be.

A pilgrim now, I evermore
  Through foreign lands must stray;
My God, and Lord! I but implore
  Thy presence on my way.

The faith so openly proclaim'd
  I will not blush to own;
Though heretic I may be named,
  Or life itself atone!

In fetters I could glory too,
  For Jesu's only sake;
And this must prove my faith is true,
  Against the charge they make.

Our Psalms and Hymns seemed now to sound much more delightfully and majestically, than they were wont to do in the temples made with hands. *We* had certainly great cause to sing, " To God alone be thanks and praise!" since we were not worthy of the favour shown us, in being made the instruments of causing his Zion, the ancient, holy, and excellent Lutheran church, thus

> Must I go forth in deep distress,
>   I will not shrink from woe;
> And God, for that, oh! will no less
>   Be my good Friend, I know.
>
> Lord! as thou wilt, so do to me!
>   Still stedfast I'll remain—
> Gladly will I submit to thee,
>   With patience under pain.
>
> Should I go forth in God's great name,
>   Then, though all else shall fail,
> Yet there's a prize, believer's claim,
>   A heavenly crown I hail!
>
> My God! but only lead me where
>   Thy word is not denied;
> Early and late my heart shall there
>   In full content abide.
>
> In this low vale of tears, if I
>   Yet poor awhile must live;
> God will, I hope, in realms on high,
>   A better dwelling give!

J. L. F.

Translated from Der Lutherische Pilger aus dem Norden. No. 13, for June, 1839.

to manifest itself as we descended the stream, as superior to its foes, in the sight of the ignorant and the scoffer. But such was the will of God, at a period and in a country, where many imagine that they no longer need the gospel.

But, to return to our voyage. We stopped the first day at the village of Nettkow, where we waited for Brother Fiedler, and the next day sailed through Crossen. The bridge at that place was filled with numbers of people, drawn thither by curiosity; some of whom ridiculed us, while others testified their astonishment, as we passed beneath the bridge. Meanwhile the police had taken measures to preserve order.

We now directed our course to Frankfort on the Oder, and reached the village which lies opposite the first sluice, on Sunday; having left Tschicherzig on the Friday, the latter part of June, 1838. We were enabled to hold divine service that day, quite undisturbed, and with all its rites—a privilege of which we had long been deprived. Our sailors were also very decent people, who took no offence at it, as is sometimes the case with the worldly-minded; and from their saying that they felt it to be an honour and a pleasure to bring us on our way, it was evident that they were by no means destitute of feeling. Thanks be to God for this also!

The second Sunday of our voyage was spent at Berlin, where we arrived on the Saturday. This was my native place. On entering this celebrated metropolis that day, with many others of my brethren, to regulate several matters respecting our voyage, I did not at all feel as if it were my native city. My heart, like those of my Lutheran companions, was no longer at home in our fatherland. Such was also the Lord's will, who seemed to lead us past the world and its glory, as it were with our eyes closed; for many of our brethren confessed that they "did not wish to dwell in a city so full of vanity." Expatriation is then an easy matter, and that which is otherwise impossible, becomes practicable. But let none suppose that this facility in parting with all the conveniences of life, arose from blunted feelings; on the contrary, it was the gift of God, and a proof how many had suffered from distress of conscience.

On Monday morning, we were conducted in our two vessels through the many bridges of the metropolis by a custom-house officer. Curiosity, astonishment, ridicule, and occasionally sympathy, at our singular emigration, were here again depicted on the countenances of the spectators. We left Berlin towards evening, accompanied by a tolerable number of brethren resident there, on board our vessels, past Charlottenburg to Spandau.

We thought it right, on such a long and dangerous voyage, when we were obliged to commit ourselves so very particularly to the Divine protection, to raise our voices in harmonious lays to the honour of our Redeemer, even at that place; I mean, near the tents on the Spree, where the higher classes generally take refreshments during their concerts, in the summer season. We know not what they may have thought on the occasion; we believe, however, that our hymns were not without a blessing. Our Berlin brethren took their leave of us, amidst tears and benedictions; we wished them also the blessing of the Lord; and it was only when the sun was about setting that we lost sight of them.

Our vessels hove to at Spandau. Several kindly-disposed individuals were present at our evening service; amongst whom were some soldiers, who wished us the Divine blessing, and took a fraternal and countryman-like leave of us, regretting that " the Lutheran church was thus compelled to emigrate."

The next day we passed Potsdam, the weather being very fine; and on the following we passed through Brandenburg, and then sailed past Rathenow and Havelberg to Wittenberg—the last Prussian town upon our route. It was Sunday upon our arrival there; we received quick dispatch, and the custom-house officers were extremely kind toward us. We had here also the pleasure, as previously at Frankfort, to see the two other vessels, with our brethren on board, following us.

We had now left the Prussian territory and sailed down the Elbe through part of Hanover and Mecklenburg, and in three days had the pleasure to see before us the city of Hamburgh—that city from whence we were to set sail on board the

Prince George (then lying at anchor there,) for a distant part of the world. The sight of this ancient, commercial, and powerful Hanse town, has really something attractive in it; and when our companions reflected how powerful this city once had been, and how much liberty in many respects it still enjoys, and how, on the contrary, the ancient Lutheran church in the most powerful of the German states was compelled to commence its wanderings in the wilderness—they felt, on the one hand, strangely enough at the sight of this ancient bulwark of German power and magnificence; whilst, on the other, they entered the vessel with joy, and with a feeling of confidence, that the Lord in his mercy would protect his church.

At Hamburgh we met with our dear Brother Heyn, who was already known to us, as well as many other estimable individuals, the recollection of whom will ever be pleasing to us, and on whom we continually implore the Divine blessing, for the unfeigned christian affection which they manifested towards us. At the last the Saviour's words will certainly be fulfilled; " Whatsoever ye have done to the least of these my brethren, ye have done it unto me!"

Our ship, the Prince George, as already noticed, has arrived at Hamburgh from London. It was now provisioned by Mr. Flaxman; and on the 6th of July, we sailed down to her in our vessels, which, though large in their way, were small compared with the gigantic Prince George.

We removed our goods into her, and took up our quarters in the place assigned us between decks.

During the two days we spent on board in the harbour, we received many visits. We had also the pleasure to read an article in the Hamburgh papers with reference to our emigration, and appearance in Hamburgh, written in a very appropriate, disinterested, discriminating, and pious manner; the author of which deserves our warmest thanks, in the name of the Lutheran and Christian church. The whole article was perfectly in accordance with the truth.

We also saw the two vessels, with the brethren who followed us, arrive safely in Hamburgh, before we left it. They were, however, compelled to remain there sometime longer; and at our departure, the time of their leaving was still undetermined. On the 7th of July, we prepared to set sail; and at two o'clock on Sunday morning, got under weigh along with the Bengal, on board of which were thirteen of our parishioners, for whom there was no room on board the Prince George, and were towed down the river by a steamer. Each one had now taken possession of the cabin assigned him, which he was to occupy until the voyage should terminate. We commenced it, however, gladly, and according to the will of God. At present, we did not proceed far, and were obliged to wait three days for the ship's surgeon, who was expected from Hamburgh. During this time brother Jensch's child died, and we interred it on the shores of the Elbe.

The surgeon now came on board, and our pilot took us further down the river. We reached Cuxhaven and the North Sea on Friday; and here I saw, for the first time, the mighty ocean, and its green and bluish waves, of which I had heard so much. The day we entered it was clear and fine; and it seemed to us much the same as on the Elbe. The next day some of the people began to be sea-sick, others not at all. I myself was attacked by it for the first time—so to speak as by an armed man.

The wind now rose, but was unfavourable, so that we were driven towards Holland instead of England. We again saw the coast of Holland; and our captain said, that the wind was very high, approaching to a hurricane. In spite of the sea sickness, we did not long to return home until we should have finished our voyage. However much there might be in Germany that was pleasing to us, yet we always felt as in a labyrinth, and as if our souls would be in danger of bondage, and even death, whenever we reflected on a return; and we then besought the Lord to hasten the speed of our vessel, to carry us so much the further away. The thinking Christian becomes more acquainted with his own heart on such a voyage, and is able to enter into the feelings of the Israelites, when delivered from Egyptian oppression. After a storm comes a calm; after conflict come seasons of refreshing. Such was our experience; the wind abated, and the sea-sickness of most of us abated with it.

After the lapse of three days, we were again well and upon deck, and praised God for his goodness towards us, and for not making an end of us.

However, before entering the English Channel, two of our number died; the mother of Brother Lange of Klemzig, and her husband, who followed her the next day. They were both of them aged, and God knows whether they died in consequence of the voyage or not; thus much we know, that they died happy, sensible to the last, and resigned to the Lord's will. "Blessed are the dead that die in the Lord!" and "The sea gave up its dead," were the thoughts that occupied us, whilst plunging them into the deep. If these two pilgrims were steadfast in their faith, the Prince of life will raise their bodies from the watery grave to the resurrection of life.

We now prosecuted our voyage courageously and resolutely; and after a passage of twelve days, including the three spent in waiting for the surgeon, we reached the English coast. He who has never been at sea before, and for a week together, and seen nothing but sky and water, feels much pleasure in again beholding verdant fields, cities, and their inhabitants; and thus the sight of the white cliffs of England, with its verdant prospects, caused us great joy. We anchored off Plymouth, about a mile from the town, in order to take my brother (the Rev. Augustus Kavel) on board, and to fill the casks with fresh water. My brother arrived in good health, and Mr. Angus, the

President of the South Australian Company, also came on board to see and take leave of us; which latter he did quite in the tone of a friend and a Christian.

Some of us, of whom I was one, went on shore, to transact some little affairs in the town; but there also we did not feel at home, for the end of our voyage was continually upon our minds; and we were still far from it, having only been a few days at sea. We continued at Plymouth for ten days, the wind being contrary; after which it pleased the Lord to render it more favourable, and we sailed with great ease out of the harbour, and along the cliffs of the English coast, until we lost sight of them.

On the evening of that day, which was the last of July, we were enabled to present our evening sacrifice of praise and prayer with very joyful hearts to the Lord; which was the case, not only upon the rivers, but on the ocean also. The Lord graciously overlook whatever was not sufficiently pure and worthy of him in it! The words of the three young men in the fiery furnace occurred to us. "Earth and sea praise the Lord, bless and magnify him for ever and ever!" And if there were some of the company who were compelled to exercise a greater degree of faith during the voyage, than we were called to do, yet still they were able to traverse the deep without terror, and could admire the setting of the sun on the mighty ocean, as we were also sometimes able to do. Faith, however, was still necessary; but it was our evening service that especially edified us on board the ship. The sailors were then, for the most part, resting from their labours, unless some change of wind called them again into activity. At one time the vessel sailed past remarkable countries which we were leaving for ever; at others we seemed alone in the midst of the almost unfathomable sea, and could sometimes reflect calmly upon ourselves or our brethren at home, and say with old Claudius:—

> "Look at those who live above;
> Think of them alone and love;"

or finally of our eventual and eternal rest. In short, our evening worship was very beneficial to us.

After this brief digression, I return to our voyage. The wind again became rather unfavourable, and we were therefore obliged to keep out at sea; otherwise it would have been nearer to have coasted along France, Portugal, and Spain: we therefore made a great circuit round the South of Europe, though always knowing minutely our latitude and longitude.

Being thus obliged to hasten past those celebrated countries, and when the thought occurred to us of all that might befall them, though we might never see them more, we could only implore in spirit a blessing upon them and their inhabitants. Not having the journal of our voyage at hand, I am not able to give correctly, all the dates, and can only say, that our ship was a swift sailer, and our captain attentive, sober, and active; also, that we were fortunate enough to reach the vicinity of St. Helena, in forty-five days from Hamburgh, without a single storm; whilst Napoleon, on sailing thither in an English ship, was obliged to spend one hundred and ten days on the voyage; we were, therefore, making a very favourable passage. We saw the Canrary Islands glittering in the distance; but we were not near enough to St. Helena to be able to see it; besides, our captain was fond of keeping out at sea, and disliked every landing place, because of the detention. We passed the line as quietly as if nothing had happened. With regard to the temperature, it was more cold than hot from Hamburgh to England upon the North Sea; from Plymouth as far as the latitude of the south of Spain, the warmth was likewise tolerable; and finally, all that is said about the line, as far as we were concerned, is not true. We observed, indeed, on our way from Hamburgh to St. Helena, that the sun, moon, and stars were in very different positions; and it is true, that about the time we crossed the line we saw no shadow, and had the sun directly over our heads; but with regard to the intolerable heat said to be felt in these latitudes, we did not find it to be the case. The sun is certainly more powerful there at noon, than off the coast of Spain; but none of us seemed to be injured by it: on the contrary, if I mistake not, my father, as well as some other old men, passed the time in their fur cloaks. It is true, the evenings there are not so salubrious as the summer evenings with us, and that the moon is injurious to the health: it is also improper to pass the night in the open air. I must here likewise observe that it deserves the name of a voyage, when the sun and moon stand in different positions to what they did at the place from whence a person sets out. Thus behind the equator, the new moon, on rising, appeared with its horns directed almost pointedly to the zenith; that is, it appeared almost like a couple of horns standing upright. We also gradually lost sight of all the stars we knew, and were surrounded by constellations of quite another kind; thus the Pleiades lay low in the horizon, towards the north, and are here no longer visible.

We had therefore passed the line, and were now steering for the Cape, the southernmost point of Africa. This was also in accordance with our wishes; for the traveller longs to reach the end of his journey; and who had more cause for this than we, who had been so long on the way; not indeed in comparison with the time usually occupied, but in our circumstances.*

But, before we reached the Cape, or rather the latitude of the Cape, we were driven fifteen hundred miles towards South America, and were obliged, first, to make good this large circuit. With the Lord's assistance, however, we reached

* This alludes to the two years detention, while the Prussian Government was refusing to give passports. EDITOR.

this remarkable division of our journey; and had now as cool weather as it had previously been hot; so that our circumscribed quarters were no longer so oppressive. The Lord also, now sent us strong and favourable winds for nearly a fortnight; so that we began to believe they would carry us direct to Australia. For though the distance of the Cape from our landing-place in that country, is from six to seven thousand miles, yet the passage is frequently made in four or five weeks, the wind being very often directly aft, and the course straight across the sea; whilst eight to ten weeks are frequently required for the first half of the voyage.

In short, with the exception of occasional contrary winds, this part of our passage was very rapid; and on the 30th of October, we had the pleasure of seeing the first point of Australia. "God be thanked," we exclaimed, simultaneously; whilst those who were well-informed amongst us, knew, from the sun's course, the direction in which we were pursuing our voyage, and from comparing the charts, that the land we saw just emerging from the sea, was indeed Australia— that distant country, to reach which so long a voyage is necessary—one of the longest which can be made by sea; for the voyage to the East Indies is not any longer. He only, who has made such a long voyage, without being a professed seaman, can fully feel how happy we were, after having, under Divine protection, traversed so great a distance. We now beheld the rocky coast of

Australia, as we had three months before seen that of England; and the country which we Germans were to exchange, perhaps for ever, with Europe.

Who could ever have thought it! The strange ideas which crowd upon every feeling mind at such an exchange, are too many to be mentioned here; they would fill a letter of themselves; certain it is, however, that it was the Lord who ordered it. And though the merchant, for the sake of gain, undertakes long voyages, and visits distant countries, yet this is a very different affair. He may, indeed, be under the Divine direction, because he is of use in the world; and trade may be the vocation to which God has appointed him; but still it is not so strange to him, as we emigrants feel it to be, on removing to such a distant land. In the latter case, the honour and church of Jesus was concerned; and it is obvious how the Lord has appeared for us.

We now sailed along the south coast of Australia; and might have accomplished this part of our voyage, (about a thousand miles) in a week or even in four days, could we have proceeded at the rate of twelve miles an hour, as was sometimes the case; but a very contrary wind caused us to be three weeks before we could reach our destination.

The last two days, our captain deceived us, for the first time, respecting our distance from the end of our voyage, and I should certainly have done the same in his place. For while we thought we were still five hundred miles off, we found, on Friday morning, at ten o'clock, that the coast of KangarooIsland was in sight, which lies only a few miles from South Australia, although a hundred miles from Port Adelaide, where we were to land. It was a beautiful morning, and our captain, who had never been to Australia, was highly pleased at having hit so correctly the straits between the continent and the island.

Our voyage might now be considered at an end; for what are a hundred miles compared with twenty thousand, which we had certainly traversed on our voyage, in one direction or another? Yes! my brethren, we worship at this distance from you—you in Europe, and we in Australia yet it is the Lord's land, and God's earth; both have their advantages and disadvantages. The wisdom of God always occurs to me, on comparing Australia with Europe. Trees, plants, animals, &c. are of quite a different kind here, to what they are there. Their variety, indeed, as Schubert, the naturalist, writes, is not surprising; since he says there are few different kinds of plants, and hitherto we have found it to be so.

But I have not yet reached Australia with any account of our voyage. On Friday, the 18th of November, above mentioned, we sailed between Kangaroo Island and Australia, and saw this island almost the whole of the following day, keeping Australia also continually in view. On Saturday afternoon, we sailed past the wreck of a vessel; and learned from some persons who were still upon the wreck, that the ship had come from Sydney, which is a thousand miles off, with goods and passengers; but had here run upon the sandbank, and lost the greatest part of her cargo, and some people. One man had lost £900, which constituted his whole property, and with which he had intended to trade at Adelaide. The captain of the vessel was ill on shore at the time. Such might have been our case, if the Lord had permitted us to pass the place in the night; this idea was impressed upon us all.

Oh, how the Lord measures out the path of the children of men! How easily he can make poor and rich, can kill or make alive! The Lord certainly has the world more in his power than we imagine, although it may not seem so; and though the free-thinker may suppose himself the author of his own happiness, we Christians, if we are conscientious, certainly do not become a farthing richer in the world than the Lord pleases: but our daily bread, which we implore in the words of his Son, must be given to us. And such has always been the case; and if it be well pleasing to God to give his people more, and cause praise to be ascribed to him, who will prevent him?

On the Saturday, above mentioned, we sailed n good spirits, direct for Australia, which we saw before us; and at noon on Sunday, reached the point where we wished to anchor, that we might send to the town of Adelaide, for a pilot to conduct the vessel into the harbour. This was a day of rest after our long voyage; a little foretaste of the rest the soul will enjoy, when it shall at length arrive, not at an earthly, but a heavenly port.

My brother, the Captain, Mr. Flaxman, and another, went on shore, and proceded to Adelaide, which lies about six miles from the coast. The Governor resides there, and the town is the rendezvous of most of those who emigrate. It is only lately founded, and is so situated, that in circumference it is about the size of Breslau; its palaces are, moreover, still of wood and clay; and only a few brick buildings are commenced. But in time it may become a handsome town; and as the harbour is not far off, the road being daily travelled by teams of four, six, eight, ten, and twelve oxen; it may be expected to become at length a considerable place of trade, if the province can furnish exports.

Our messengers soon returned to the ship with the olive branch—with Australian productions, foliage, and a couple of birds which had been shot. We were the more pleased with these articles, as they afforded proof, that we were again near mother earth, where things live and grow.

The next morning the pilots conducted our vessel into the very narrow, serpentine harbour, which is difficult of access, and where there were still signs of vessels which had been wrecked. The immense chain cable was now brought out with great demonstrations of joy, by the sailors. and the anchor cast into the sea. We felt very differently on witnessing this, to what we did on seeing it near Hamburgh, for the first time. We could do nothing but fervently bless and praise God, who had prepared our path in the sea, and had borne us as on eagles' wings ; and we do so still, though much too little ; for what is man!

We were now obliged to think of discharging, and landing our goods and ourselves, and did so willingly, and this was gradually carried into effect. We first of all removed to a place called Port Adelaide, which lies about a mile from the harbour. We were there obliged to build huts, since each of the inhabitants possesses only his own little house.

An Englishman offered his field for that purpose, which was the more desirable, since we found upon the place, a shed which was being built, which we covered with linen, and could therefore occupy it as a large family mansion. He did this gratuitously, on hearing that we did not come there merely for gain, but in consequence of persecution.

The English also permitted us to make use of their church, which, though only built of boards, we found very serviceable, and which we were at liberty to occupy every Sunday and Wednesday from the time of our landing, free in every respect, from the visits of the police officers, and from paying for them. Oh that our hearts were only sufficiently incited to praise and pray; for there is liberty in Australia!

True it is that many a householder with his little ones, and many an aged man has been compelled to seek this liberty at a great distance; yet the Lord has permitted them to find it; and on this occasion it is my prayer to God, and earnest wish, as well as the desire of us all, that the Lord may cause our brethren in Prussia to find a free altar, point out to you what you ought to do, guide you with his eye, graciously regard your persecuted state, and send help, either by removing you hither or elsewhere.

Your situation is a difficult one; for when I imagine to myself what the magistrates would have said, had I returned them my permission to emigrate, and said, "I wish to remain here, but to hold worship in the Lutheran form," I shudder; because I know—not that this would have been wrong, for it cannot be called wrong for a person to regard his conscience and his peace in the land of his nativity, as his own property in all godliness and honesty—but because I know that I should then have trifled with them, and that certainly no regard would have been paid to me.

Blessed therefore be the Lord for ever, for having helped us! He has done so to the amazement of our enemies, and has safely brought our vessel hither. Though the wind may have occasionally been tempestuous, and the vessel have laid deep on its side, yet we were never afraid of being lost: this fear the Lord took away, so that in this respect we were on a par with the sailors themselves. We justly concluded, that if God permitted a number of individuals to peril their lives for his gospel's sake—(for could liberty of conscience have been obtained in any other way?)—he who is gracious and merciful must take notice of it, and either put the scorners to shame by granting us a prosperous voyage, or, if he suffered us to perish, promote in this manner his glory, which was our object, and the good of our souls. The Lord does not forsake his people, for his Son's sake; and he who desires to betake himself even only to the outworks of Zion, will find that the Lord is his shield. Oh, though it be true that we are not worthy of his aid, yet he hath chosen us and we obey his voice in some degree.

Here, in Australia, no one scoffs at us hitherto. It seems almost as if Prussia—on which the Lord has shed such a bright light—contained the largest number of scoffers. This we have sufficiently experienced. The most illiterate individual in the towns and villages of that country, if he can do nothing else, can violently blaspheme the word of God. How degrading to the German character! and how perverted must the mind of that individual be, who can treat a quiet and humane fellow-countryman and neighbour with blackguard vulgarity, solely because he honours God. I should not have written this if the case were not so, as you all know it to be.

But such a scorner is a most pitiable individual; and I can explain to myself the cause of his mockery, somewhat in the following manner. Supposing such a person to stumble upon one whom he regards as devout, he may perhaps feel his conscience affected by the Spirit of God, and think within himself, Such an one ought I to be. Now, the louder the monitor speaks to his soul, and the less inclined he is to obey it, the more strongly and strikingly is the picture of his own wickedness, in comparison of the pious man, placed before him; and where repentance does not result from it, the basest mockery is manifested. How often have I experienced such treatment in my native land, and the town where I last resided; although I never took any notice of it, and have often been astonished at the existence of such degeneracy. May the Lord forgive these scoffers! Our only object in mentioning them here is, that if this should meet the eye of such an one, he may perceive that his conduct does not appear to be very magnanimous. Thank God! the savages here are not such degraded characters, and probably scarcely know that it is possible to be so depraved, although they are certainly in a very pitiable and neglected state. Boast, if you will, of having driven the Lutheran church fourteen thousand miles across the sea! a voyage of this length is certainly preferable to living in such society. All our friends and neighbours, however, except such as derided us, are still remembered by us, and that with constant affection.

Our voyage was now finished, and you will wish to hear how we are situated here. But before I enter upon this, I must mention something more respecting the voyage. Whilst it lasted, fourteen of our number died; seven children and as many adults. I will not enquire whether their death was caused by the voyage. God alone knows. If, with their relatives, they went forth for the truth's sake,—if this be the case, as it certainly is, and if they lost their lives in consequence of the fatigues of the voyage, their death is sacred, and they have become more or less martyrs for the truth. With respect to some, this may be said with truth, and the Lord has inscribed their names in his book. But that the Lord can also afford strength on the sea, is equally certain; for he has favoured my brother and myself, with permitting our aged father, now seventy-three years old, the patriarch of the party, and our equally aged mother, to survive the voyage; and my father was not even sea-sick. But this will be believed with difficulty; and the town-clerk at Wollstein, when my father applied along with the rest for a passport to leave the kingdom, grieved me with expressing the opinion, that "the fish would eat my father," &c. But it is remarkable that the Lord confounds such mocking Goliaths, who would eat up his people, and who blaspheme his name.

Now as regards our residence and outward circumstances; we removed at Christmas and the week following, to the place of our destination, which lies to the left of the town of Adelaide, and about a mile and an half from it. We have there taken one or two sections of land on lease for seven years, where we shall build houses and cultivate the ground. The soil is very good, rather clayey, but, at present being summer uncommonly hard, and must be tilled during the rainy season. We have, however, already attempted to dig up our garden ground, and sow seed for culinary purposes. How far we shall succeed by frequent watering, which is constantly done, remains to be seen. We are making the attempt.

Fruit and vegetables are high in price, because the English who reside here are mostly merchants, and not agriculturists. Flour and potatoes must be brought hither by sea, from Van Dieman's land; they are dear, and it is shameful that agriculture, which makes rich, though not without labour, should be so neglected.

Labour is here also high, and the labourer is well off, as long as the rich can pay him, or require him. But when this is at end; that is, if the colony receives no more money from England, or if no more rich people emigrate hither, who have money to spend, the people must have recourse to agriculture.

Oxen, sheep, and horses, are also brought from Van Dieman's land. The former are used for draught; but the harrows are so heavy, and so many are yoked to them, and so little effected, that the sight is laughable.

The kangaroo, the only game in Australia, has been driven by the Europeans a hundred miles into the interior; and he that wishes to have one must fetch it from thence. However, I have once seen a kangaroo. It is an animal like a hound, and of a foxy colour. Except whales and sharks, we saw no marine animals, and these only at some distance, mostly to the south of the Cape. We also saw birds as large as a great swan. They are called Albatrosses, and the captain caught some of them.

There are here also fowls and swine; also many dogs, though but few cats. There are here likewise singing birds, but of a different kind from those in Europe; also many parrots and cockatoos.

With regard to the vegetable kingdom, the plants here are few; the trees consisting chiefly of what are called gum-trees, which are not suitable for building. None of the European species grow here. There is, however, a kind of tree which seems like an oak, the wood is very fine and beautiful, burns well, is cheap, and may be had almost for nothing. But we require no firing, and have had summer ever since last June, when we left Prussia. To-day it is as hot as you can have it in the dog-days.

Four weeks after we landed, the Zebra, Captain Hahn, arrived safely at Port Adelaide, and brought the second division of our brethren, from the district of Züllichau. They had lost eight by death; and both as regards the time and the weather, as well as in other respects, had made a voyage similar to ours. Thanks, praise, and adoration, be ascribed to Him who has helped us hitherto!

They took possession of the huts which we had

left, and were equally glad to be able to land. We had often thought of them on the sea, and felt impelled to entreat the Lord, for them, even as they had done for us. With regard to their outward circumstances, the Lord so ordered it, that when they were on the point of looking at some land in our neighbourhood, belonging also to Mr. Angus, with the intention of farming it, like as we did, a gentleman of the name of Dutton purchased four thousand acres in this neighbourhood, in a district which surpasses ours; and as it lies behind and between the hills, it is not unlike Swiss scenery. This individual being acquainted with the German mode of farming, was glad to meet with Germans for his tenants, and thus it was evidently ordered that each should be of service to the other. Our brethren are now engaged, and removing thither.

Mr. Dutton has promised to exert himself towards making provision for a church and a school, by pecuniary aid, and intends to found a German town there. May the Lord give his blessing to it all, and bless us, especially in spiritual things! the temporal will then also prosper.

My brother, as preacher, will be obliged to keep a horse, in order to visit the brethren; and Mr. Dutton has promised to send one shortly from Sydney, where he has three hundred of them. It is Mr. Dutton's wish, which is saying much for an Englishman, that we should constitute a regular German colony.

Finally, three weeks after New-year's day, the Catharina likewise commanded by a countryman of ours, arrived with the third company of brethren, from the Duchy of Posen. The Lord has also conducted them safely across the sea. They were one hundred and thirty in number, and had only lost four on the voyage. They sailed from Hamburgh a fortnight before Michaelmas. They were, therefore the same time on their way as we. On leaving Hamburgh they experienced much sympathy from the dear christian friends in that city, who took leave of them in a very solemn manner. The Lord bless the dear Hamburghers, and reward them on the day of recompense, for the kindness shown to his members!

The outward circumstances of the brethren, who have last arrived, remain still unsettled. It is said that they will probably be placed near us. The Lord will provide for them! They have now landed with their furniture, and occupy our old huts. There are now, therefore, about five hundred Lutherans from a little district in Prussia, here together in South Australia. Whether the Lord will send more; or, in other words, whether other Lutherans will be compelled, by continued persecution, to emigrate hither, we must leave to him. It is not our wish to persuade any, nor to dissuade them. The affair itself, and voyage, are important things, and if the matter be determined and the hand of the Lord is seen, it is also evident that we may trust ourselves in his hands, and then the voyage will be according to his will, and will end well.

. . . . But I am now obliged to close, and to refer you to my next letter. Receive, therefore, once for all, my salutations to you all; for time does not permit me to name you individually, but I nevertheless include every one of you. Let this letter circulate among you all. Gladly would I write more, but the vessel is departing.

In the name of the brethren, your brother in the Lord.

FERDINAND KAVEL

Translated from the German, by J. D. L.

CHAPTER XII.

HIGH TESTIMONY RESPECTING THEM, FROM THE SOUTH AUSTRALIAN GAZETTE.

The following extracts, which appeared in the South Australian Gazette, for June 8th, 1839, will serve to show the high estimation in which the Lutheran emigrants are held in that country. It was written on the occasion of their having voluntarily assembled in a body, to take the oaths of allegiance to Queen Victoria.

Our attention having frequently been called to the German emigrants, we have great pleasure in inserting a document, proceeding from our respected friend, Pastor Kavel, expressive of their sentiments, on the late occasion, when, in a manner so creditable, they came forward heartily to testify their attachment to the British Crown. The address is characteristic of that ardent, and deep-seated enthusiasm, which so distinguishes the German nation. It overflows with grateful feeling towards their benefactors, while it breathes not a murmur against the Sovereign to whom they formerly owed allegiance, and by whose ordinance alone they were necessitated to abandon their dearest ties of kindred and country. It is also so modest in abstaining from allusion to their own claims, that we cannot allow the opportunity to pass without adverting to the advantages resulting to the colony, from our German brethren. There are now at least three villages located with German families, besides a number of individuals, of both sexes, employed as servants among the colonists. We have heard but one account of their conduct, and it is the most satisfactory possible. They are uniformly found to be conscientious and industrious in service, regular, sedate, and capable of applying themselves to many different kinds of labour. The females are adepts at almost every household and rural occupation; and the men, (whatever may be the appropriate trade which they more immediately profess,) are all useful labourers, in digging and fencing; and many of them excellent in building, sawing, and carpenter work. In labour of this kind they are often preferred to our own countrymen, who, in many cases, might do well to imitate their patient and enduring habits. In the Mount Barker district, in particular, they have been found invaluable, where the settlers, without them, would have been reduced to the alternative of bringing up labourers from the town, at great expense, or of being dependant on the tiersmen, who by their generally intemperate and profligate habits, are unfit to be received into any establishment.

The Germans of Hahndorf, have been drafted out in parties among the settlers, and have assisted in making stock-yards, fencing, breaking up ground, and building houses. They rise early, and work late—are moderate, and easily contented as to food and accommodation—are cheerful and pleasant in their intercourse with fellow-labourers—and even during the hours appointed for relaxation, will offer to bake, or do other useful things about the station. But the most prominent characteristic of all, is their piety. In every act they acknowledge their God—when they rise—when they are at meals—and when they go to sleep. At the end of the week they like to return to their own village, to join their congregation; or when this cannot conveniently be done, the parties at adjoining stations will meet to celebrate divine worship, and " sing the songs of Zion, in a strange land." Striking is the effect of these Teutonic accents, rising amid our solitary places! Here, however, they have that liberty of conscience which was denied them at home, and they can live contented, in spite of various privations. They express themselves simply, but emphatically on this—" What more has man to do," said a very intelligent elderly member of the community, " than to labour, and to pray without ceasing?"—*(Beten und Arbeiten)* They labour and pray accordingly, and look with faith to receive the blessing of God upon their toil. Surely such a people deserve to be happy!"

ERRATA.

Page 69 line 17 *for* 1836 *read* 1838
110 .. 4 .. 1839 .. 1838

Page 141 end of Chap. XI. *for* "translated from the German, by J. D. L." *read* translated from the German, by Samuel Jackson.

www.ingramcontent.com/pod-product-compliance
Lightning Source LLC
LaVergne TN
LVHW081353060426
835510LV00013B/1802